STREET TALK

STREET TALK

The Great Flood and Other Stories from a River City

The Columns of Dan M. Luzadder

Edited by Hannah M. Cowden

Briton Publishing, LLC
810 Eastgate North Dr., Suite 200
Cincinnati, Ohio 45245
www.britonpublishing.com

ISBN 978-1-956216-18-9 Hardback
ISBN 978-1-956216-16-5 Paperback
ISBN 978-1-956216-19-6 E-Pub

Editor: Hannah M. Cowden

Briton Publishing books are distributed by Ingram Content Group and made available worldwide.

CONTENTS

Prologue

A Journalist's Journey

The Fort Wayne News-Sentinel is a part of that city's history now. The afternoon newspaper was founded in 1833, when "The Landing" along the Maumee River was a vigorous, major transportation center throughout northern Indiana, a hub for shipping produce and products. The paper survived under local ownership for nearly 150 years, but went from local to corporate ownership in 1980. As foundational changes in technology swept the news industry in the late 1990s, changing the newspaper business forever, the paper was downsized. The loss of staff followed readership and revenue declines and finally its doors were shuttered by its last distant media owner; and, it ceased publishing in 2017.

There was no funeral.

The paper's pinnacle of journalistic achievement was the 1983 Pulitzer Prize for General Local Reporting, awarded to a largely cohesive staff of reporters who had been covering the city of three rivers together during the late 1970s and early 1980s. Reporting on the Great Flood of 1982, even as many were evacuees themselves, their work was judged the best in the nation that year. Among those honored was the paper's news columnist, Dan Luzadder, whose columns covering the flood were later collected in college journalism textbooks recognizing his work as a model for other journalists.

Luzadder was hired in 1977 for the newspaper's copy desk, the only job open in a lingering economic downturn, but some months later was called into then-editor Ernie Williams' office where, as he later recalled, the editor declared him "the worst copy editor I ever hired!" He'd been an aggressive, colorful police reporter before his hiring on the mostly quiet copy desk, and was admittedly challenged by spelling. But he defended his work and asked the editor 'why?'

"Because," Williams told him, "you rewrite everyone's copy to sound like you! I've got 30 reporters in this newsroom, and I want them to sound like themselves!"

Luzadder said he asked quietly if he was fired.

"No," Williams told him "...you're our new columnist."

"Street Talk," as he named the column, was more hope than reality when launched two weeks later, since Luzadder had no sources out on the street. But over time that source network grew and he learned to sniff out stories where no one else was looking. They were stories about common people in their common lives and, eventually, Luzadder said, the 'street talk' emerged. Along with it came his desire to be on the inside of untold stories. It would become a hallmark of a long journalistic career.

Collected here are columns that Luzadder wrote between 1978 and 1983, some of which were aired on public radio; he left the News-Sentinel in 1984 for a place on the investigative team of the state's largest newspaper, the Indianapolis Star. He would later spend a decade with the Rocky Mountain News in Denver, and then move to freelance writing for the New York Times, the New York Daily News and for New York and Los Angeles magazines. He eventually turned his investigative skills to books.

Yet, he always insisted that his Street Talk columns, however flawed, were a highlight of his career.

Here are some of those stories he wrote in the city where three rivers come to confluence, and where his colorful columns described life as it was in those days, in the heartland of middle America, in another era.

■ Hannah M. Cowden

Part 1

Sandbags and Sirens: The Great Flood, a City in Peril

The Great Flood has stood as perhaps the highest profile media event to occur in Fort Wayne in the last century. There were others, including the attempted assassination of a civil rights leader, that made national news. But in 1982, as the city fought the Great Flood and saved a historic neighborhood from destruction, national television crews walked the sandbag dikes and told the story of disaster. President Ronald Reagan came to encourage the battle-weary sandbag volunteers, and local military reservists went days with little sleep or rest in the pitched battle against the forces of nature. Dan Luzadder was one of the evacuees during the flood. His dispatches, with those of other reporters, came from within the midst of sandbag crews and among those whose homes were lost and those whose homes were spared. His words, some collected in college textbooks on feature writing, still bring those scenes to life more than four

decades later. Here are his contributions to that historic staff coverage. –
Hannah M. Cowden (HMC)

A FITFUL NIGHT FOR THOSE
WHOSE DREAMS LIE UNDER THE RIVERS

It is midnight Sunday, at the moment of this dispatch, and the streets are quiet. But, in the heart of the city, hearts are breaking.

Homes sit under water. Cars have been swallowed up. Houses sit dark and empty of occupants as furniture floats on the floors.

The lapping, slowly rising waters make an insidious sound on clapboard walls. But otherwise, the evacuated areas are quiet. And all is calm.

This is what the eye sees, the ear hears. Yet, as the city's sandbag heroes lie down to rest tonight, only turmoil greets those made refugees by the flood of '82.

They sleep tonight on lumpy, unfamiliar cots in rooms with linoleum floors. In the church centers, this thankful and restful sleep comes only when anxiety succumbs to fatigue. And hundreds more bed down in strange houses, waiting for word of more rain.

At this hour, it is said, 3,900 have been forced from their homes. More are of the old working-class neighborhoods, which lie along the west banks of the city's three rivers.

It is mainly here that the city swallowed water and spit up refugees. Boat people. Tired Marines, firefighters, and volunteers came after them, helping the cumbersome and reluctant into small aluminum crafts, ferrying them to the high ground, where the other transportation awaited.

Now, at midnight, the evacuated parts of the central city sit in the dark, their power cut, the gas off, all semblance of normality gone.

Those who made a stand in time – fighting with sandbags and hasty earthen dikes – have only to wait for the rivers to crest. Their homes are spared, for now, and their confidence returns. They sleep in their own beds tonight. But they wonder too, how much more water the city can take? And rain lurks in the night sky.

To the west of the rivers, the heartbreak is the hardest. The loss greatest. Where the Maumee and St. Joe only licked the levee tops, residents climbed floodwalls hourly for inspections of the water's leading edge. They looked for signs of hope. Where the levees held, they found it. Where they did not, hope drowned like a rat.

A thousand stories are being told tonight by the refugees. Things they saw and heard.

One thinks of a house on Van Buren Street, where sunlight sparked springlike off a yellow picket fence. An elderly couple waits in the front yard of their little yellow house. The gentleman sits on a yellow chair on the walk, a cane across his knee. His wife, her yellow hair now white, stands watching the curious walk by. They are a Rockwell print. A yellowed photograph, out of place.

A block away the water inches up the street toward them. The woman speaks only broken English. Her husband only nods. Worst flood. Ya. Worst flood. How high is it coming? A shrug. Will they have to leave? A faint, uneasy smile. Who knows, she says, who knows?

Along the levee of the Maumee, where the river runs its widest and deepest, the whispering water rolls in the dark. Few people come and stand on the levee under the street light. It is unnecessary now. They feel safe.

In the pocket like Lakeside neighborhood, nestled in the bend of two rivers, the waters did not win. Here there is elated relief. The sleepless anxiety of Saturday night is over. There are no cots, no anguish over flood-damaged lives. They escaped the flood. But it came so close.

Now, just after midnight, as the city slips into sleep, its 3,000 refugees housed and fed, there are still two worlds. The wet and the dry. The highlanders and the lowlanders. Two cities, separated by swollen rivers and closed bridges. Two kinds of luck. Good and bad.

Tomorrow, it is hoped, the cresting will come. The crest comes, the water recedes and the homeless return to the little sorrows of lost mementos. And to dig out, once more.

But that is tomorrow. Tonight, there is still that uneasy sleep of the weary; unfamiliar beds, the strange emptiness of a battle – part lost and part won. Tonight, in the heart of the city, hearts are still breaking. But the worst is over. The streets are quiet. And all is calm.

THE CHILDREN SAVED OUR CITY

Pemberton dike. It's famous now. Famous and secure in this city's history. A place where they dug in, where the troops met the odds, and the odds were broken. Where they pulled victory out of defeat, turned fear into courage, stood in the jaws of the beast, looked it in the eye and spit. The world knows. It's where the heroes of Lakeside made their stand. And won.

It was slop out there Wednesday night. Like walking in a pigpen after a storm. Brown water ran beneath the streetlights and crews changed in an endless stream. It was cold enough on Pemberton Drive to turn your nose red. Yards full of muck, no place to sit but on sandbags, everything wet, and nothing warm but coffee.

In the early evening darkness almost every face you saw in the street belonged to a kid. A teenager. Nearly half of them were young women and girls. But you had to look twice to see that. Side by side in the sandbag lines, gender disappeared behind muddy sweatshirts and slogging boots. Just hands, hanging on to the only hope left for Lakeside. The situation on the Pemberton dike had worsened as the rivers moved toward their crest Wednesday. School kids, guided by a handful of military advisers and teachers, were walking into a quickening crisis.

By the time night fell on St. Patrick's Day, the leaks were running through the dikes in finger-sized streams. Kids clambered off the buses to be greeted by a sea of despair. The scene was eerie. White lights made colors stark. The quiet neighborhood, in a matter of hours, had become a battlefield.

The noise of the pumps at Pemberton and Cody ran at one pitch, full tilt, throwing runoff into the backwater in a foot-wide stream. Over the top of it all you could hear the kids chanting and shouting to each other. Full of blood. Noisy. Urging themselves to work faster. Trucks rumbled up the street. Air brakes hissed. The chatter came out of the yards, and the sandbags made a "thunk, thunk, thunk," as they slapped the dike.

Up and down the street the muddy water ran in rivers. It pooled on sidewalks and rushed down driveways, coming down to the street to run fast into the gutter. It ran toward the manhole where water gushed into a ring of sandbags and spread underfoot, inching up the curbings. You couldn't see where it came from. But it was there. You could hear it. Too many leaks, not enough sandbags, not enough time, and the Maumee still rising. The water inched, and the seepage under Pemberton dike gained.

This was at 10 p.m. on the night of the great battle of Pemberton dike. It was a pitched battle, for defeat meant a wall of water would come down that dike and smash anything in its path. Houses, cars and human beings.

But in the face of it, there was no talk of defeat. The kids, bused in from the Coliseum, stood in long lines and kept their voices up. They shouted everything they said. Hand to hand, sandbag to sandbag, driven by some unknowable force, they kept it up. Backs aching, muscles pulling. And spirits high. But the real battle hadn't even started yet.

"It's the children who are saving us," a woman said to her friend as she filled cups and watched from across the street at a coffee and sandwich table. She was smiling. It was bad then, but from the street you couldn't see how bad. In a little while, there would be no smiles. The crisis was coming.

"This is a dangerous game," a man said as he stood looking through the darkness at muddy yards. It took more than courage to stand beneath a wall of sandbags and clay. With no warning, the dike could turn to a 9-foot wall of water.

Sandbag after sandbag passed slowly through many hands. The plastic was rough on the skin as gloves fell off in the mud. Nearly shoulder to shoulder the heroes stood up against fatigue. They fed on adrenaline. Tension ran the lines. Strain showed in the young faces.

At 10 p.m. the leaks were dangerous, but by 11:30 fear was spreading. Cops with bullhorns swept into the immediate neighborhood to clear it of people who hadn't heeded evacuation warnings. The bullhorns rattled: "Leave your houses immediately. You are in immediate danger."

Radio calls crackled to the Coliseum where hundreds more teenagers, fresh volunteers, filled the green plastic sandbags. Under the street lamps the Pemberton dike was a sieve. Word filtered up and down the dike, crew chief to crew chief. They told the kids on the line. Things were getting shaky. They might have to retreat. Everything hung in limbo. Then the word went out. Retreat.

The kids broke ranks and started across the street. They fell back to Anthony Boulevard, slogging through mud and then walking tiredly along the dry sidewalks. A sense of defeat threatened.

"What's happening?" a girl asked another. "Are we giving up?"

Her friend only shrugged and moved off to find someone who might know.

The leaks which had driven the troops away from the fight were expected to widen fast. But they didn't. Not right away. And as minutes crawled by, a slender thread of hope hung to be grasped.

There was still time for one great stand. One last desperate effort. The decision came suddenly, and like battle-scarred veterans the crews started back into the fray. Teenagers, slogging back to the heart of battle, going at it quickly now, and then, out of the darkness, coming into the neighborhood behind, the reinforcements arrived.

Pemberton dike was suddenly a beehive. Brave young men and women plunged into the mud. They threw sandbags just to stand on. The air was electric with impending danger. In the heat of the battle, the chants grew louder. Courage. Courage. Every bag thrown echoed against the falling dike.

The ground wasn't safe anymore. An excavating truck, laden with sandbags, drove into a yard and began to sink. They could not get it out, so they worked around it. Nothing stood in their way.

Seven hundred strong and stronger they came. At first it looked like the dike had been breached. Someone said a three-foot hole had opened up. Trucks of clay lined up to dump, and the sandbag trucks fought for space in line. Bag after bag came down. The supervisors kept the lines tight and the throws short, so stackers could slap the bags fast to the earth. "Thunk, thunk, thunk," bag after bag, until they numbered thousands.

It was getting late now, long past midnight. Cold mud and water slipped into boots. Up the makeshift dike the kids went, eye to eye with nine feet of water, enough to send houses off their foundations, enough to drown people if they didn't work hard enough, fast enough. They worked like madmen. Like heroes.

The dike watchers stood in the white lights in the street, amid the roar of pumps and the rumbling trucks, and held their breath. It was a battle for the property and lives of 15,000 people, the entire Lakeside neighborhood. A pitched battle with hope on one side, destruction on the other. They stood for what seemed like a lifetime on the crest of this frail bubble, and then, as if by the sheer force of will, the tide began to turn. The leaks slowed.

Elation spread through the ranks. Silent cheers of the heart were raised and prayers were answered. Muddy smiles broke out and lit the faces of children in the white light. Fatigue took over. Giddiness came.

The kids started to laugh again. They hit each other on the back. And they grew up, lives forever changed.

It was 3 a.m. now. The heart of the crisis passed. The dike sat precariously, waiting on more work. Fresh troops of kids marched onto the sandbags, keeping the work up through the dark, into dawn, and all-day Thursday.

Even now it sits, Pemberton dike, a jellylike sham of a barrier, resting on the sandbags that saved a neighborhood, resting on the courage of a few hundred kids who saved millions of dollars of property, and probably lives.

No matter what happens now, no matter what the rain does or how soft the dike gets, no one can take away from those who fought the victory they won. Their hearts were in it, they snatched victory from the gaping jaws of defeat. And with the world watching, they showed what spirit this city is made of. They are the heroes of Lakeside. Part of a legend, now and forever. The kids who saved a city from destruction.

A SEASON OF WINTER DISCONTENT, THEN CRISIS

The snows came hard on the winds of winter and piled deep in the city yards and streets. Bitter cold raced through the town and frostbite was as common as stocking caps. Seventy-below windchill. Day after day, weekend after weekend, we sat, housebound by the cold, restless with cabin fever.

We got tired of seeing snow, finally. Every inch that fell was another blanket of awareness. We embrace the first, warming days of March as children embrace the end of school. Coats and gloves came off even when the temperatures hovered in the 30s.

When it was clear the great thaw was certain, that there really would be Spring, after all, wariness lifted. We saw sunshine. And never had a city wanted sunshine so badly.

All this was in our minds and hearts in the days before the great flood of 82. It was a hard winter. The hardest of winters. But we came through it all right. And though we were bright with the promise of Spring, it was winter that wasn't through with us.

There was no question a flood was coming. Such talk began long before the last snow fell. Sidewalks were like mazes in the city. Streets were bound up by walls of snow. When the melting came, the water had to go somewhere. We knew how it would go.

Throughout the long winter, the rivers froze and thawed. In the deepest cold, steam rose off them like fog. We were always aware of them. They lay flat and stark and sometimes snow covered. But they were not our enemies. Not yet. Just curiosities, viewed from automobiles on trips over slippery bridges.

We had our puddles in late February. A false thaw. Water trapped between layers of deep snow stood on sidewalks and froze again. You could skate on the streets. Cars locked up solid to the hubcaps in the ice. It seemed endless.

But then came the March thaw, and the snowbanks shrank like violets in the sun. Runoff streamed into icy gutters. The nights stayed cold and the rivers clung to their banks, far below highwater marks. Each melting day, seem to lessen the chance of flood.

Still, we knew it was coming. Those who suffered in the floods of '78 complained and street crews dumped massive snow piles and flood prone Lawton Park. Some got angry. They plagued City Hall with calls.

But in the weeks before the great flood, official meetings were held. The situation has been assessed; plans mapped. Some said the city was ready. People seemed reassured.

The first week in March brought clear days and warmer air. It was glorious. Who could think of flooding while sun warmed winter were souls and coats gave way to jackets? The danger was inching forward. And we knew it. But we had been lucky before. And after such a winter such a cold how could a flood be so bad?

The National weather service has issued a warning. Flooding in the Maumee Basin was certain. The rivers would leave their banks in the lowlands. But this was not news. We had grown accustomed to warnings in our long winter. One elderly woman whose home suffered in the Spy Run floods of '78 began clearing her basement. She gave away canned fruit. No other place to store it. The crisis was drawing near.

By Wednesday, March 10, temperatures were in the 40s. Just to be safe, Emergency Preparedness Director Tom Rody had asked high school students to fill sandbags at the city garage. Only a few responded. The city had 55,000 empty sandbags stockpiled. The students filled 2,500 of them.

On Thursday, March 11, the rivers were already climbing. Some rain fell and temperatures rose to 45 degrees. But at night, the puddles froze again. For the last time.

On Friday, March 12, things started to happen. The St. Mary's, which had already crested two weeks earlier in Decatur at 20 feet with no ill effects here, now stood at 21 feet downstream. Six feet above flood stage. The St. Joseph was thawing fast. Swollen with runoff, the rivers hurried through town.

That Friday it got warm. By midnight, 54 degrees. The runoff from the snows of our hardest winter ran in torrents. The time had come.

Mayor Winfield Moses had called task force members together Friday afternoon. They reviewed plans to fight a flood. In the afternoon, Moses toured the city's dikes alone in his car. When he went to bed that night, it was for a troubled sleep. The city was poised on the brink. Everyone was waiting.

At 1 a.m. Saturday the weather service delivered its most ominous message. City Transportation Director Carl O'Neal found out about it at home. Thunderstorms were on their way. He sent engineers to walk the dikes. All seemed stable.

At 6 a.m. Friday, the Maumee had stood at 15.3 feet. By 3 a.m. Saturday, it was at 19 feet. By 6 a.m. it was over 20 feet. Five feet over flood stage, and still rising.

In the low areas, we knew what was coming next. Those closest to danger began to pack. Radio stations interrupted programming in the morning to plead for volunteers. Warnings flashed on television screens. Sandbaggers were needed. Urgently.

The 30 students who arrived at the city garage at 9 a.m. were followed by more volunteers. But the work went slowly. Trucks filed out, looking for trouble spots. There was no question now that sandbags were needed immediately. For parts of the city, it was already too late.

All day Saturday the rivers rose. Water bubbled into the streets from sewers. Swinney Park flooded. Water lapped over the roadways and covered the ground. It inched into snowbanks. Geese, migrating, settled into the backwaters of the park. People began to leave their homes in droves.

The Emergency Operations Center in the City-County Building came to life early on Saturday. Firemen dispatched into threatened neighborhoods warned residents to evacuate. But as the waters rose, time had expired. With little notice, little time to prepare, the Nebraska neighborhood was under the gun. There was no choice. Forced evacuation.

There was no stopping the rivers now. Not for Nebraska. The St. Mary's seeped over its lowest dikes. Hastily laid sandbags could not hold the water back. The lines broke. A dike gave way near Sherman and Superior and water surged into the neighborhood. Emergency teams called for rescue boats. No time to raise the furniture now. No time to make peace with the rivers. They were the enemy. And the enemy swept like shock troops into the shaken neighborhood. On Elm Street, water was nine feet deep.

So, part of the battle was lost. Marine reserves, on a weekend training exercise, abandoned plans and pulled strings to be relieved for duty against the flood. More than 80 of them waded into the fray. First, they manned the failed dikes. Then, slogging through icy water, they evacuated those who held on until the last. Sandbags were useless. The race was lost. The water poured in.

More than 1,000 people were forced from their homes by early Sunday. Some at first refused to leave. Others didn't have time to take a change of clothes. Refugees streamed into evacuation centers opened at Precious Blood Catholic Church and Trinity Episcopal Church. The refugees came in wet, bewildered and homeless. They were met with kindness and hot food.

Firemen had cut utilities as the neighborhood battle was lost and part of the city plunged into darkness. Cars were enveloped slowly in the dark water. Some disappeared. Pets clung to porches. Rescuers came for them.

Throughout the long night the rest of the city sat stunned by the sudden drama. A few hundred volunteers shook of the lethargy and drove into the ravaged downtown. They lined up in the City County Building cafeteria for assignments. There was great confusion. And not enough room.

By now officials said the flood at our doorsteps could be the worst in our history. Worse than the killer flood of 1913, when the rivers crested at 26.1 feet, when all of Lakeside was submerged. Could it be true? No one knew. The city held its breath.

But the rising waters slowed and by Sunday morning there was new hope. The crest predicted for 4 p.m. came on time. At 24.3 feet, half a foot higher than the flood of '78, the water stabilized.

Now the volunteers arrived in earnest. Residents with businesses at the edge of the flood turned out in the sunshine Sunday carrying pumps to fight the waters. It looked as if a corner had been turned. As if perhaps the worst was over. But the enemy was not sleeping. The waters churned on.

Governor Robert Orr declared the city and surrounding county a disaster area on Sunday morning. People walking along the dikes in the Lakeside and Lawton areas, eyeing the high water, gazed overhead as the first military helicopters chopped the sallow air. In these areas yet untouched, where sandbags crews fought the rising St. Joseph to a standstill, some of the tension subsided. The relief was to be short-lived.

Monday the weather service brought more bad news. Storms were on their way. Once again, the city waited. Clouds made rain seem imminent. But no rain fell. A quarter of a million sandbags were already piled on the dikes. But now came first word of a new problem. The dikes, in place for 69 years, had begun to weaken. They leaked.

Most of the thousands who fled their homes found shelter with friends. But hundreds went to the evacuation centers. Donations to help the stricken arrived. Red Cross units from around the country went on alert. And the national media found Fort Wayne on the maps. They too poured into the city.

Now we watched ourselves on television. Network news, morning and evening. Live hookups. Bright lights. The fight was shaping up and not a minute was missed. By late Monday, we knew the rains could not hold off forever. The nation knew it too. Volunteers swelled to the thousands as the gray skies held back throughout the night.

Tuesday morning, the rains came.

The situation was stable at midmorning, but by noon it worsened. It rained harder. A storm sewer blew near Lake and Randalia. It was the first sign of serious trouble at Pemberton dike. Lake Avenue was closed. They pumped water the water back into the sea behind Lakeside Junior High.

Scattered schools and flooded businesses closed around the city Tuesday. School officials feared students might be cut off from parents and homes if the dikes began to crumble. And high school students were needed in the sandbag lines.

The mayor's plea for federal assistance Sunday had touched a chord. Word filtered down that President Reagan, stumping for his policies in western states, would stop in Fort Wayne to see the floods firsthand.

By midafternoon the sun came out again. The temperatures soared. It hit 60, then 70, then 72 degrees. The air grew heavy and humid. It had its own earthy, unsettled smell. A tornado warning went out. And then, as reporters waited for Reagan's plane to land, a twister dipped out of the sky to the south of Baer Field. What next, we wondered. What next? It was on everyone's lips.

For some of the President's appearance at Precious Blood and his presence on the sandbag lines bolstered confidence. For some, it was a sham. Reagan, in borrowed galoshes, threw sandbags for the national television cameras. But then he was gone. And the flood was not.

Now the rains of Tuesday were felt. The rivers were on the rise again. This time, they told us, the rivers would crest over 26 feet. The highest dike in the city was 26 even. Disaster was already upon us. Calamity was all that was left. Orders went out from City Hall: Evacuate Lakeside and Lawton.

The news was a flood of sorrow for the neighborhoods. They had weathered everything up to now. Floods hadn't touched them since 1913. Disbelief settled in. Tensions ran high. Families began the backbreaking work of carrying furniture to second floors. The dikes were "weeping," water seeped beneath them. You could see it in the street.

The staging site for the great battle to come had been shifted to the Coliseum. More sandbaggers streamed in to replace those exhausted by the herculean effort being raised. Blacks, Whites, Vietnamese, Latinos. Young and old. It made no difference. They were one people with one goal: to save a city. They came in hordes.

Tuesday night and Wednesday the Lakeside neighborhood empties. By Wednesday night the streets were eerie, damp and dark. Most everyone had fled. A few stayed behind. The city waited once more. The waters were still rising. All over the city, 10,000 had left their homes.

Now the battle had reached a fever pitch. Pemberton dike, the weakest link in the chain of dikes, was leaking like a sieve. Pumps battled water in the street, and teenagers, with schools closed, rushed into the fray. Thousands of them. Teenagers, the last great hope.

All Wednesday the battle went on. National Guard troops patrolled abandoned streets and helped the Army Corps of Engineers guide the fight on the dikes. But it was the teenagers who threw the sandbags. Hundreds of thousands of sandbags were all that stood now between Lakeside and a wall of water that would bury the neighborhood. Still, the crisis had not been met.

Late Wednesday night, all hell broke loose on the Pemberton. Three-foot holes opened up in the dike. Hundreds of sandbaggers were forced to retreat before reinforcements arrived. Trucks and loaders poured into the neighborhood east of Anthony Boulevard, dumping clay over sandbags as the dike eroded before the eyes of courageous volunteers.

Slogging through the mud, the teenagers fought all night. What heart. What stamina. Sometime before dawn, they beat the water back.

The battle of Pemberton dike was the turning point in the great struggle. On Thursday rivers crested at 25.8 feet. Only inches of the dike remained. But the Pemberton had turned to jelly. And the teenagers, guided by tired engineers, rebuilt it entirely of sandbags. Braced by the backs of garages and homes, the muscles of youth, the dike held.

All day Thursday they piled sandbags onto the weary dike. Even the rains of late Friday morning could not turn their victory around. The ground gained was ground won. And the victory would stand.

By Friday afternoon, the dikes were quiet. The cresting rivers inched slowly down. But the crews gave the enemy no respite. They continued to pile sandbags along St. Joseph Boulevard. The Edgewater dike, too, had weakened and leaks streamed into the gutters at Morton Street. Again, the sandbag crews had their way. Again, they stemmed the tide.

Saturday, people began returning to their homes in the Lakeside neighborhood. Guardsmen still patrolled the streets, demanding identification from residents, and their vigilance paid off. Looting was held to a minimum. The city began to relax.

Across the nation those who had watched the great struggle raised cheers for the courageous teenagers and volunteers who saved their city. Television and newspaper carried the story around the world. The heroes of Lakeside were hailed as lionhearted, stalwart, brave. Their place in this city's history secured.

But the heroism was scored by sadness. Not everyone survived unscathed. Not the refugees from the Nebraska neighborhood and surrounding areas. The damage had climbed to $20 million. Many were left homeless. Basements collapsed. Camera crews and reporters followed them on the agonizing journey home to see what was left. For some, it was virtually nothing.

By Monday thousands had returned. For most, their homes were safe and dry. Lakeside survived almost untouched. So did most of Lawton Park. Others were not as fortunate. River Haven, so inappropriately named, was inundated. Much was lost. The debris left scars in the yards, the streets and the mind.

Many refugees who fled their homes found water standing in living rooms and kitchen. The mud that dried caked and cracked. Linoleum buckled. Wood floors pulled way from the subfloors. Appliances were damaged. Property destroyed. Clothing ruined. And the scrapbooks and photos, those bits and pieces of the past, too important to be trusted to memory, were gone. Somewhere down the block, or down the river, they had disappeared. Gone.

Some say we could have been better prepared for this flood. But it an easy thing to say in hindsight, harder perhaps in the heat of the fight. One-fifth of the city stood under water. But four-fifths did not. Schools closed, but they reopened. Damage was done, but it will be repaired. And the spirit of the city, its outlook, its pride in itself, shown through. The people of this city showed something to the world. They showed it how to fight with simple tools. With hands, and heart. It was all they had, and they gave it all.

In all the eight days of trial, not a life was lost here. Not a person was seriously injured. We held our own, gathered our wounded and shielded them. In the hearts and minds of the kids who saved us, there is a spirit that did more than stop a flood. Maybe it puts us on a new road, a higher ground. Maybe it stopped to the floods of despair from a city hurt by other things, by internal strife. Time will answer that.

For now, the digging goes on. The rebuilding remains. But it will be done with enthusiasm, by a town knit closer by what we learned. We stood together in our darkest hour. One city, hand in hand. And the tide was turned.

Part 2

When the Lives We Live Make News

Mixing it Up in the World of Violent Crime

The Parker Whiting murder plot unfolded on Luzadder's watch as he worked the streets of Fort Wayne. He learned of it before the police, and helped lead them to the perpetrators. It would be the sort of front-page stories he would be recognized for on numerous occasions throughout his five-decade-long career. The paper published the columns as a series; the stories won statewide awards for reporting. The stories open with an editor's note on the series as it was unfolding in 1979. –
HMC

A CONSPIRACY TO MURDER: HOW CRIME WAS EXPOSED

Allen County Police detectives – acting on information supplied by News-Sentinel Columnist Dan Luzadder and Earl Harts, an alleged "hit man," – arrested two men early Tuesday afternoon on charges of conspiracy to murder a retired, prominent and wealthy Fort Wayne businessman.

Arrested were Frank Whiting, 48, Coldwater Mich., and Robert Hagler, 40, 1832 Webster St. The two men face charges in a plot to kill Parker R. Whiting, 81, father of Frank Whiting. Parker Whiting has been a patient at the Byron Health Center for the last two years.

Frank Whiting and Hagler appeared in Allen Superior Court Misdemeanor Division on preliminary charges today and received continuances to Dec. 26.

Luzadder and Harts contacted police Sunday night with initial information on the plot, handing over a secretly made tape recording of a meeting between Harts, Whiting and Hagler. Harts had been offered $5,000 to smother Whiting in a privacy room at Byron Health Center, using two towels left in the room by Frank Whiting.

Police tape recorded a final meeting Monday afternoon in which the murder was set to be carried out at 7 o'clock that evening. Whiting, who is reportedly in severe financial trouble and would have profited from his father's death, slipped out of police surveillance Monday afternoon. Efforts to find and arrest him Monday night failed.

Luzadder and Harts led police to Whiting early Tuesday afternoon, and police made the arrest. Parker Whiting was not harmed. Both Hagler and Whiting were charged with conspiracy to commit murder and are being held in the Allen County jail on $50,000 bond each.

Parker Whiting, who had been under police guard since Monday afternoon, was the former president of Fort Wayne Union Stockyards and founder of the Fort Wayne Charity Horse Show.

Luzadder, in a three-part column beginning today, recounts the six days between the first attempt to farm out the murder contract, and the arrest Tuesday, as he watched it unfold. Below , is his story. - The Editors.

Well, it's over. Frank Whiting and Bob Hagler are in jail. The bond: $50,000. The charge: Conspiracy to commit murder. And the victim, Parker R. Whiting, a once-prominent businessman in this city, is still alive.

This is a strange and bizarre tale. It is about a "hit man," who is a friend of mine, and about a man who valued money more than the life of his own father. It is a family tragedy. And a rare glimpse into the inside of a plot to murder a man. This is the whole story—from the inside looking out.

It started last Thursday afternoon. I came in late that day, and was thumbing through the newspaper, checking things out, when the phone rang. It was Earl Harts, a long-standing friend of mine in this town who has advised me on matters from larceny to protocol in dealing with all manner of courts in Allen County. He had something cooking, he said, and he thought it was hot.

"I think a couple of guys want me to kill someone," he told me. I'd heard outrageous stories from Earl before. I was in no mood to listen.

"Come on Earl," I said. "Are you serious. Murder somebody?"

"Damn straight, I'm serious," he said. "At least that's what I think they want. I'm going to find out at 2 o'clock this afternoon."

Earl Harts has been involved in a lot of things in his life. He's got a reputation as a jailhouse lawyer, and he's been in and out of trouble as long as I've known him. He's got a reputation some people in this town look down on. But I never heard him talk about a crime like murder before.

"Who's the victim supposed to be?" I asked him. It was getting near lunchtime and I was thinking about heading for the Acme Bar.

"Don't know yet," he said. "Don't know nothin' yet."

"Where are you going to meet them?"

"Out here."

"Well," I said, "if these guys are serious, you better be careful. You don't know what they might be into."

"I'll be careful," he said. "I'm gonna' put a tape recorder in my pocket and tape the whole thing. I'll call you if I get it."

When I hung up the phone it didn't occur to me that 24 hours later, I'd be slipping a .38 under my pillow when I went to sleep, or that four days later paranoia would take over and force me out of my own house. But it was all in the cards.

When I got back to the office Thursday afternoon there were two notes on my desk. Both said call Earl immediately. One was marked urgent. It was underlined three times. It said to go straight to his house. The notes were 20 minutes old. I headed for the car.

Earl was working in the lot outside his garage. He crawled into my car and we headed for his house, a short distance away. He was being very quiet. Hardly a word was spoken. Inside the house, he had the tape recorder sitting on the worn, Formica countertop in his cramped little kitchen. The sun was coming in through the west window showing up the dust hanging in the air. He flipped the button on.

"Listen to this," he said. It was deadly quiet inside.

The tape began to play and I heard the sound of three men's voices. The tape was a little ragged at first, hard to hear. But then the voices came floating out, clear, calm, frightening. Earl had gotten into a car with two men. The conversation started there:

BOB HAGLER: "Frank, this is Earl. Earl, this is Frank."

FRANK WHITING: "I'm glad we could get together."

EARL: "Yeah, uh-huh."

FRANK: "Earl, we got a case. We, got a case here. The target (pause) is in his 80s. He's got a pacemaker. It's a case where, there's nothin' left. He's got a pacemaker; the body and mind are just deteriorating around him. The guy's given up. But the motor is running."

EARL: "Yeah, I know what you're sayin'. What's he sick with?"

FRANK: "Well, old age, mainly for one thing. But the machinery's just breakin' down all around. Heart attack, stroke, a light one, left arm damage from that. Diabetes, borderline. Hernia against the heart. He had a spell here a few weeks ago, was in a coma for three days. He's on borrowed time."

All of a sudden, my doubts were gone. Earl stood back at the corner of the room and watched my face. He could see the look of recognition on it. We knew what was coming. Earl shook his head slowly, side to side.

FRANK: "The thing is, he's not like some guy that says, 'oh-boy, let's go out and get something done today,' you know. The ball game is over. But the heart's going. He's in a wheelchair."

Frank began to explain the layout of the Byron Health Center where the as-yet-unidentified victim, the man in the wheelchair with so little time left anyway, had been living for the past two years. He described the traffic flow, the availability of getting to him, the ease of getting out. All the details, point by morbid point. Then he began to get to the meat of the matter.

FRANK: "It'll have to be kind of (pause) a pillow job. They have what they call a privacy room. This guy likes to sit in the chair, use his feet to pedal around. He likes to look out the window. They have a privacy room. You go down around the station there, down a little hallway, then there's a door that says do not disturb, door's closed. Privacy room..."

FRANK: "So now you have an area that's secluded and undisturbed. Uh, how long can you hold your breath?"

There was some garble, some speculation on how long, actually, an elderly man could hold his breath. All three men talked. Then Frank spoke again.

FRANK: "So we're talkin' a quick situation."

EARL: "What's the possibility of gettin' the hell out of there in case somebody does catch you at it?"

41

FRANK: "Well, that's good too. But they won't catch you at it, because the door is shut. Case in point. I put two towels a week ago in that room on a table. They're still there..."

EARL: "Don't they use it?"

FRANK: "This is it. When that door is shut, for uh, for residents and their gusts only, do not disturb. (Garble), restricted (garble). You're talkin' a five-minute situation, or less. Whatever it is. We're also talkin' about five (pause) thousand dollars."

So there it was. Earl looked at me hard. The offer had been made. It was no small sum. Probably more than Earl made slinging scrap iron in the whole year. A lot more. He shook his head again. "Can you believe it," he whispered.

FRANK: "So, all right. He goes. I'm on the team that backs it up. My legal tells me, (pause) I ask him these questions because we had to think about 'em, where we gonna put him, what kind of a service would he want, what kind of a casket, all those things, even though we don't like to talk about 'em, they got to be talked about."

There was a little garble. Frank said he talked about the will with his attorney because he wanted to know about getting an advance on the money to handle funeral expenses when his father died of natural causes.

Frank indicated an advance on his father's estate was possible. Then he went on. His voice, cool, calm, matter of fact.

FRANK: "So, if the action takes place, (brief pause) the best timing is about 2 or 2:15 in the afternoon. We'll say that we put him in the ground Saturday or Sunday, if we can go that quick, we're talking about probably Friday (for the payment on the contract) or Monday the following, before Christmas."

A truck went by in the background, obscuring a small segment of tape, a few seconds. Talk resumed.

FRANK: "You have a great amount involved as far as money goes on his (the victim's) part. Over the years, he's dissipated a good part of the estate."

EARL: "So he's not mentally competent, though?"

FRANK: "No. If you went in today, and I introduced you as a friend of mine, you went back tonight, he wouldn't know you... But the point is, as far as the game plan goes, if I took you out there now, and we just walked though so you're familiar with where to go, and how to get out, so you don't pass the same area twice... because the traffic flow is such out there, they wouldn't even pay any attention to you."

EARL: "Yeah, well, I've been out there once or twice myself."

FRANK: "I could take you through this afternoon, and I could show you where everything is. He likes to go for a ride... so, when you know, where your guy is, you go out tomorrow afternoon, or whatever your timetable is, you can go up and talk to him and say hey, by golly, Betty's comin' and we're gonna take a little ride. He acts different toward Betty than he does toward me (pause) or, uh, his other son. Betty's his wife. So, say, Betty's comin' and we're gonna meet her. You just take him out, down the hall, about 30 feet, and down to the privacy room, another 10 feet. There's no problem."

EARL: "Well, why don't you pick me up tomorrow afternoon and we'll look it over."

There were a few more moments of tape and then it ended. They had agreed to meet at Irene Byron the next afternoon at 2 p.m. Earl shut off the tape and looked at me.

"They mean it," he said. "These boys are serious."

"Who the hell is this guy, and who's the guy he wants killed," I asked. I was still having a hard time making the thing seem real.

"I don't know yet," Earl said.

"Did you get his license plate number?"

"I couldn't. The tape recorder was falling out of my belt, I was afraid I'd drop it. I just walked away."

I knew we had something. And now I knew we had to do something about it.

"What about the cops," I said.

Earl shook his head. "You think they're gonna' believe me with my reputation with just this?" He laughed softly. "Besides. We don't even know who these guys really are yet."

Murder Conspiracy: Suspicion Grows as Plot Unfolds

Frank Whiting, 48, Coldwater, Mich., and Robert Hagler, 40, 1832 Webster St., appeared in Misdemeanor Court, Wednesday morning on preliminary charges of conspiracy to commit murder. Their cases were continued until Dec. 26. Both were arrested Tuesday by Allen County detectives Graham Foote and Joel Working, after a plot to kill Whiting's father, Parker R. Whiting, 81, Byron Health Center, was exposed by News-Sentinel Columnist Dan Luzadder and the alleged "hit man," Earl Harts. Luzadder's three-part account of the murder plot, as he watched it unfold from the inside, began Wednesday with details on a secretly tape-recorded meeting between Whiting, Hagler and Harts. During that meeting Harts was offered $5,000 to kill Parker Whiting by smothering him. This is part two of Luzadder's three-part account. - The Editors

For now, the cops were out of it. We didn't have enough information. Earl was convinced they wouldn't take him seriously. Not with his reputation.

Earl stood at the counter of his ragged little kitchen, rewinding the tape. I looked out the window. I was beginning to get the first of many uneasy feelings to come. I wondered what it took for a man to offer $5,000 for a murder. How desperate was he?

"You've got to protect yourself, here," I told Earl. "This recording is pretty incriminating."

"I thought we'd make copies of the tape," he said. "You can keep one, so will I. I think you should go out tomorrow to kind of back me up in case anything goes wrong."

"All right, fine. What we need to do is get a picture of this guy when you meet him, and get his license plate number. That way we can find out who he is."

"The guy he wants killed has to be his own father," Earl said. "Did you hear the part on the tape where he said the guy acts different around Betty, than around him and his other son. I think he slipped up there, a little, you know?"

"Do you think they're suspicious at all of you?"

"Well, I don't think so."

"Do they know anything about you?"

"Bob does."

"What's his last name?"

"I can't think of it right now. I know he's black and he owns Poor Boy's Furniture Store on South Calhoun Street. Me and him have had some deals together. He buys stuff from me. Hell, I don't even know why he picked me out when he set this up for Frank. He don't even really know me that well."

I stood in the tiny living room of Earl's house and looked out the window. It was only about 3:30 p.m. My car was sitting in the drive.

"Any chance they'd be watching your house," I said, "just to be sure you weren't going to the cops or something."

"I don't know. But they haven't got any reason to be suspicious yet."

Earl and I talked. We speculated on what we needed to take to the cops to stop the plan, on what could happen and what might have happened.

Earl could have turned down the contract flat. But he didn't and now, at least there was a chance to save Parker's life. If Earl had the guts to keep the thing going.

"I'm not afraid of them," Earl said. "I've been into a lot of things, but I'm against killin'. I never mess with anybody's body. I wouldn't do that. They don't know me very well, if they think I would."

We needed another tape recorder. The one Earl had was too big and bulky. He was going to wear a suit Friday afternoon when he met Frank at Irene Byron for the walkthrough. He needed a recorder that would fit unnoticed in a shirt pocket.

"We got to get him to talk about money," Earl said. "If we get him to come up with front money, then we got him, don't you think? That would really make a case on those two."

I sat down and called the office. In vague terms I told them I was in the middle of a murder plot. I needed a small tape recorder. I said I'd be back in an hour or so, could they have it ready? They said they could.

Late that night, after dark, I slipped back to Earl's house. It had started to work on me. I was watching side streets near Earl's house for the dark blue Pontiac he'd described from the first meeting, in case they might be watching his house. It wouldn't be healthy for either us or Parker Whiting if they got suspicious. We didn't know a thing about them. I had gotten Bob's last name. Hagler. But that's all we had.

We sat at Earl's kitchen table, under a steamed-over window and copied the original tape twice. I slipped one into my pocket and left. I saw a dark car sitting a block away, but I dismissed it.

It was a long night. Over and over, I played the tape on a tape player and listened to it with the noise level reduced. It sounded sinister, final, matter-of-fact. This was a human life Frank was talking about. His own father. But he sounded so cold. Mechanical. Businesslike.

Friday morning, I brought the tape to work. I'd spent most of the day and night Thursday dealing with the situation and trying to tie an unrelated column together. Now I played the tape for Ernie Williams, the editor, and managing editor Joe Sheibley. They agreed we should run with it. Find out who Frank was, get the name of the victim. The hour of the meeting was drawing near.

Photographer Greg Dorsett and I loaded gear into my car and headed for a preliminary meeting with Earl at Hall's Hollywood on Lima Road. It was 1 p.m. I had the micro tape recorder with me.

Earl and I sat in his van outside the restaurant and went over details. I'd never seen him in a sport coat before. He was nervous. And there was a problem. The tape recorder only had a 20-minute tape on it. And it beeped when the tape ran out. It was too risky. He was afraid it would go off while he was still with Frank. We decided to have him go in without it. Dorsett and I would find a place to park, nearby, unobtrusive, and he would shoot pictures with a telephoto lens of the meeting. I'd get Frank's plate number. With that, the identification would be easy.

Earl was already in the parking lot of the Health Center when Greg and I arrived. We drove slowly through the lot, up and back, checking to make sure Frank wasn't already there in the dark blue Pontiac. The parking lot was full. We couldn't get a clear shot from there. We decided to cross Carroll Road, in front of the Children's Home. Maybe we could shoot from there without being seen. Then, by circling while they were inside, we could get the plate number. We didn't think about Frank having a backup, too.

We'd turned the corner on Carroll Road driving slowly, looking for a place to stop, when we spotted the dark blue Pontiac. It was in the shadows, in front of the Children's Home. As we passed, it pulled out of the drive to the edge of the road. The driver sat there, watching us. We pulled into a drive, turned around, headed back. We didn't know what to do. We didn't want the driver to see our faces. I pulled into a lane behind the Home. We felt whoever it was had spotted us, had spotted my car, anyway. They acted suspicious.

The Pontiac pulled out onto Carroll Road, stopped and waited until we got past the buildings. Then it eased slowly up the road toward the intersection.

"You want to go inside the Youth Services Buildings," Dorsett said. "Maybe it would be a cover for us."

We parked, got out and went inside. Greg made small talk with the receptionists. I watched out the window as the Pontiac sat for several minutes, then pulled out and over to the Health Center parking lot. It toured each aisle among the crammed lot, then pulled past Earl's van and parked facing Lima Road. No one got out. Dorsett and I walked back to the car.

We didn't know for sure if we'd fooled them, but we were sure it was Frank or Bob in the car. Maybe it could have been anyone. But the way they moved, and looked, someone was suspicious of something. We decided to play it safe.

I started the car, pulled out and turned back toward town on Lima Road. Dorsett kept an eye on them. At Dupont Road we turned right to circle behind the Health Center. We planned to come up from the other side. Dorsett would get out, move to a place of cover on foot, and try to get his shot from there. The person or persons in the Pontiac hadn't gotten out to approach Earl's van. Maybe we could still catch sight of them.

We turned on Bethel Road, behind the Health Center, and again on Hathaway Road. Then something strange happened.

I'd slowed to a stop at the railroad tracks, just as a turquoise Ford convertible crested the hill in front of us and came to a stop. A black man in a green jacket climbed out of the driver's seat, walked into the middle of the gravel road and tried to wave us down. We edged over the railroad tracks, down the incline and up to within 50 feet of him. He was holding one hand in the pocket of his bulky coverall-like pants as he moved toward the edge of the car. When he did, I pulled past him. There were three other blacks in the car. They watched as we slung past. The man in the road jumped back into his car.

Paranoia was starting to grow. We pulled up to Lima Road. I was wondering out loud.

"You don't think those guys might be covering for Frank and Hagler," I said.

Dorsett shrugged. He was looking out the rear window of the car, trying to see if they were following. We turned onto the highway and got up to speed. They were nowhere to be seen. There was a rush of adrenalin going through us both.

"Maybe Frank saw my car at Earl's house," I said. "If I can get a license plate identified, maybe they can too. It's possible they know what we're up to."

Ahead of us we saw Earl's van pulling from the Health Center lot. As we sped by, the dark blue Pontiac was still there. One man inside. We couldn't even get a make on him. We'd blown the photographs, the license plate and everything. We suspected we'd been spotted. Maybe they even knew who we were. Earl turned off up ahead. We didn't want to follow in case someone was watching. We headed back to the office with the bad news.

There was no answer when I tried to call Earl for the next hour. I didn't know if they had gotten onto him, if he needed help, or if the magnitude of what these men were planning had only mushroomed in my mind. There were only four people who knew the real details of the conspiracy. Frank and Bob and Earl and myself. We didn't even know Frank's last name. And now there was this.

I started looking around for a car to borrow. If they had spotted me, they would know my car. If they were watching Earl, I didn't want them to see my car near his house. I found a car and drove out, not knowing what I'd find.

Earl's van was in his little gravel drive, and his dogs were barking outside. I knocked four or five times and there was no answer. I called out his name, loudly, several times. Finally, I heard him stir inside. He'd been asleep.

"What the hell happened to you?" he asked. "Where'd you go?"

"I think they might have seen me," I said. "Did Frank make contact with you at all?"

"Yeah, I saw him."

"Was he in the dark blue Pontiac?"

"No. He came up in a light blue Pontiac. Baby blue. With a white convertible top. Didn't you see him. Where's the pictures."

"We blew it," I said. "That dark blue car you described was cruising the area and we thought they were suspicious of us. We tried to circle around. By the time we got back, you were leaving. We didn't get anything."

I explained about the other vehicle trying to stop us. We discussed the possibility they were onto the whole thing.

"Frank didn't act nervous at all," Earl said. "I went in, he showed me everything. I saw the old man. But I couldn't get his name. I know where his bed is though. We can find out. I'm supposed to go back out Sunday and case the joint by myself."

"What about his license plate. We didn't get it. I'd sure as hell like to know who he is, especially if he knows who I am."

"I got it," Earl said. "I scratched it into the dashboard on my van."

He went outside and came back with the number. I wrote it down, copied down a map of how to get to the victim's room to try to get his name, and left.

I felt better. Maybe it was all imagination. And maybe not. Back at the office I tried to get a friend to "run" the plate number, to find out who owned the light blue Pontiac convertible. There wasn't anyone around willing to do it. I tried a friend out of town. No luck. It was too late on Friday night. I knew I couldn't do anything on Saturday. There wasn't anything to do but wait, and speculate what Frank and Bob might know. That night, late, I went to a friend. Maybe it was just paranoia. But I borrowed his .38. A security blanket. Just in case.

Earl called early Saturday morning. Nothing was new. He said he was going out late Sunday afternoon to look around at the Health Center. He said he'd try to get the name. He called again Sunday morning. Still nothing new. No contact from Frank or Bob.

"I don't think they suspect anything," he said. I began to feel foolish. I took the heavy, chrome .38 out of its hiding place and unloaded it.

The sun had gone down, the temperature was falling. I was reading when the phone rang. I knew it was Earl. He had some information. I didn't know it would turn out to be the key piece that would really get things rolling.

"The man's name is Parker Whiting," Earl said. "He wasn't in his room. But I found his name. Frank is supposed to be out of town in Michigan. He's supposed to be back tonight or tomorrow. Did you get the plate run yet?"

"No luck," I said. I grabbed a directory. "No Frank Whiting in the phone book. But maybe Frank isn't his real name."

Earl was silent.

"We'll check it out in the morning," I said. "Are you supposed to meet him tomorrow?"

"Supposed to set it up with Bob," Earl said.

"Okay. I'll call you tomorrow."

Even as I hung up the phone I was restless. Now we really had something. The name of the victim. Parker Whiting. I knew he had money. That was Frank's only visible motive. Money. Now I couldn't sit still on it. I had to find out what I could. Maybe, I thought, by checking out the newspaper's morgue file, I could learn something else. It was worth a try.

It was cold when I got outside. I'd had my car in the garage over the weekend, just in case someone was looking for it. But I'd dismissed most of those fears now. Nobody knew. I'd convinced myself of that. Still, I carried the .38 out into the night and tucked it into the rubber strap beneath the seat.

I started out for Dorsett's house. I thought I'd tell him about it first and get him to go out cruising with me, trying to spot Frank's car. We thought we had his name, but we didn't know where to find him when the time came for the cops. If we could sew that up, maybe it would help.

I'd gotten to Dorsett's house, but as I got out of the car, something was bothering me. It was kind of late to stop without phoning. I decided to go to the office first and research the whole thing. I got back in the car and pulled out. When I did, there was a car behind me.

It pulled close as I turned down College Avenue and made for Jefferson Street. It was right behind. It spooked me. I kept an even sped, then turned right on Jefferson at the light. It didn't follow. I began chastising myself.

"Paranoia," I thought. "Rampant paranoia."

I drove on down Jefferson Street to Fulton Street and made the turn. I drove the three blocks to the newspaper office, and pulled into the visitor's lot. As I stepped out, onto the sidewalk, I saw a car pull slowly into the lot at the other end. Then I did a double take.

The car was light blue. I looked closer. It had a white convertible top. It was a Pontiac. Same year. And there were two people inside.

I felt my heart skip. It had to be Frank. There couldn't be more than one car like that in 100,000. I stood by the door looking for a moment, then I slipped inside.

My mind was racing, my heart pounding as I went up the stairs. I came into the locked, darkened newsroom and made for the window. They were gone. I sat down on the desk and thought it out. Then I called Ernie Williams. I told him what had just gone down. He said he thought it was time to bring the cops in on it.

I was unnerved, but I wasn't convinced. We had the victim's name, but we didn't have any sign of money yet. We didn't know if a crime had even really been committed at that point. We didn't want to blow everything. I said I'd think about it for a while.

As I wandered around the big, quiet, empty newsroom, I moved to the windows in the front of the building. I was standing there, looking out and under a streetlight, I saw a dark blue car. It looked like the other Pontiac.

It was sitting with its parking lights on, its engine running, a few dozen feet from Fulton Street. I could see the steam from the exhaust rising into the cold air outside. That was enough. I called Williams back. He said he'd call the sheriff and then get back to me. I waited in the newsroom, listening to the gentle hum of the AP photo machine. Finally, the phone rang.

The cops were in.

Murder Conspiracy: The Last Details...Then, The Arrest

This is the last in a three-part series on how a plot to murder an aged, wealthy, retired Fort Wayne businessman was exposed by News-Sentinel Columnist Dan Luzadder and alleged "hit man" Earl Harts. Frank Whiting, 48, Coldwater, Mich., and Robert Hagler, 40, 1832 Webster St., were arrested Tuesday by Allen County Police officers. They were charged with conspiracy to murder Whiting's father, Parker R. Whiting, 81, of the Byron Health Center. Luzadder's inside story of the crime, as it developed, detailed on Wednesday the events that led to the discovery of the identity of the murder victim and of the man who planned to kill him. Today, the capture - Editors

It was 8:28 p.m. Sunday night. A detective from the Allen County Police Department was on his way to the office. I'd picked up the phone a few minutes before, after discovering I'd been followed by a car matching the description of Frank Whiting's. Then I called Greg Dorsett, one of our photographers.

"It's weird you just called," he said. "You popped into my mind just a couple minutes ago. I've been trying to reach you at home. I felt like something was wrong."

It must have been telepathy. Dorsett knew most of the story, knew I was wary. He said he was heading up to the office. He had some photos to process anyway.

It took maybe an hour for Detective Graham Foote to get from home to the newspaper office. He strolled in wearing a brown leather coat. He was tall, big build, in his mid-40s, easy going. I asked for his identification. I began to tell him the details of what I knew without going into the tape. He said that was interesting, but not much to go on. When I played the tape for him, things changed.

I told Foote about the light-blue Pontiac outside the office, and who I believed it belonged to. He called the radio dispatcher at the Allen County Sheriff's Department and took the license plate number I had been unable to run. He had it fed into the computer. In a couple of minutes, it came back. He penciled the name on a sheet of yellow paper.

Frank Whiting.

But the plate came over as registered to a cream-colored, '75 Pontiac. He asked the woman to double check. It was a mistake. It was a light-blue, white-topped convertible.

Foote asked more questions. I told him what I knew and what I believed. I told him the name of the victim. He'd heard of him. Parker Whiting. Wealthy, a land owner, prominent before he retired. He asked me for Earl's name, but I refused to give it.

"I'll have to talk to Earl before I do that," I said. He wanted it before he went to the sheriff or the department's legal advisers. I told him he'd have to wait. It was up to Earl now.

I couldn't reach Earl at that hour, so Dorsett and I drove by Earl's house. Everything seemed secure. Foote told me he wouldn't advise me to stay at home alone. I called a close friend. I didn't go home that night.

I sat up into the early morning, thinking the thing over. I remembered Earl's admonition at one point that the whole thing could be a set up. An effort by someone to get even with him. I couldn't believe that was true. But he said there were some people in town, some cops even, that hated his guts. I couldn't get that off my mind.

At 7 a.m. the next morning, Monday, I headed for Earl's house in a borrowed car. I told him what had happened the night before. He said he didn't know what to think. I told him I'd gone to the cops. That they were in it now. That they wanted him to set up the meeting with Frank, to wear a wire or another tape recorder. To get him to make an offer of money, to make some kind of payment. Earl agreed.

A few hours later, I picked Earl up at Ellies Tavern on Broadway. He was inside playing pinball when I got there. He'd parked his van out in back. It was dark inside, and Earl was a little jittery.

"You think they're wise to us?" he asked.

"We'll know when you try to set up the meeting. If they balk, we'll know something's up."

We met Foote and his partner, Joel Working, in the basement of the county courthouse, in the vice and narcotics office. A couple undercover officers were there. Foote and Earl and I stood in the foyer, discussing the ground rules. They said they needed to get a money offer, a money transaction. They had a tiny, pocket recorder for him to carry into the meeting. They set up another recorder to tape Earl's call to Hagler.

Everything went smooth. Even if Frank Whiting suspected something, Hagler didn't show it. Maybe there was another light-blue convertible in town. Maybe it wasn't even his car that followed me. Maybe he only saw my car by coincidence. I didn't believe that, but who could tell. We didn't know. But we did know Hagler promised Frank would meet Earl at a restaurant on the west side of town at 2 p.m. that afternoon.

Foote and Working staked out the restaurant an hour before the scheduled meeting. Foote and I sat in an unmarked Thunderbird in a parking lot near the restaurant where we could watch the action. Working was sitting up higher on a hill. We didn't see Earl pull in. But about 45 minutes before the scheduled meeting time, Frank's baby blue convertible pulled into the lot.

"There he is," I said.

Foote went for the radio. He called Working and checked on the two undercover cops who were supposed to go inside a half hour earlier. They couldn't be reached on the radio. So Foote sent his partner inside. We watched as Joel loped across the parking lot, his gray suit jacket flapping in the cold breeze. They were inside more than a half hour. Finally, Frank came out. He was wearing dark glasses, a brown coat, some kind of sweater vest. Foote radioed to have someone pick him up and tail him as he left. Frank cruised by our parking spot. I kept my head down. He kept moving.

In a few minutes, Earl left. Then Joel came out. He had the tape recorder in his hand. We started to play it back. The sound was a little low, but it could be heard. They talked about the money. About setting up the hit. They agreed it would go down at 7 that night.

Frank went back over the instructions. Earl said he had to have some front money. Something. Anything. Frank went into his wallet. When he came up with some bills, he told Earl how much it was Later, when Earl counted it, it was two dollars short.

Earl went downtown with the detectives later and for the next two hours, he went over his video-taped statement. Foote and I drove back to the newspaper. On the way, a radio call came from the car trailing Frank Whiting. The officers had backed off near St. Joe Center Road, and Frank had slipped away. They were afraid he had seen them. He skated out somewhere into the city. No one knew where.

Foote had already met with the sheriff and the prosecutor's office. The case was tight. They had what they needed. There were a few other details to check out and they went about them. They decided to make the arrest, get Frank first and see if he would talk. They began to research how to find him through the Health Center. No luck. They tried the family. No luck there either. Betty, Parker Whiting's wife, was away from home. Foote and Working tried to cover all bases. There was a rumor Frank had gone to Coldwater to build his alibi. They checked the Branch County Sheriff's Department.

Bits and pieces about Frank began to filter into Foote's office. Bad financial trouble. Bad checks. An eviction notice, finance trouble on his car. The picture began to emerge. Money. All money.

I sat in the office Monday night and waited. If they found Frank, Foote was to call and pick me up so I could watch the arrest. The hours went by slowly. I took the time to research. To look into Parker Whiting's background. I knew he'd been president of the Fort Wayne Union Stockyards. That he was now 81 years old. That he'd been retired since a stroke 15 years ago. The files were scant. But there was nothing else to do. Wait, and look. Foote never called.

Seven o'clock, the hour the murder of Parker Whiting was to take place, came and went. Earl was at home. The sheriff's department had placed a guard at the Byron Health Center to watch over Parker. Everyone was safe. Arresting Bob Hagler would be no problem for the cops. Now it was all down to finding Frank. About midnight I left the office and got in my car. I was too keyed up to go home. I started to cruise through the dark, empty streets. Earlier in the evening, Dorsett and I had been past Hagler's house on Webster Street. We didn't see anything. Now I cruised by again. Nothing then either. I wondered where Frank might be. It was anybody's guess.

I called Foote early Tuesday morning. If the arrest was made before 1 p.m., I had a story to get out. I wanted to get as early a start as possible. I'd been living with this story now for five days. I wanted it to be over. I was anxious.

Earl had gotten me out of bed with a call before eight o'clock. He didn't know what to do. The hit had not been made. He was sure Frank or Bob knew that. He needed to call, he said, to make an excuse. I called Foote. He said he'd reached Parker's wife, Frank's stepmother, and she had agreed to cooperate. They thought they might be able to reach Frank in Michigan, tell him there was an emergency at the Health Center, and have him come back immediately. It was a good plan. But it wouldn't work. Frank wasn't in Michigan.

Again I waited for a call. Earl phoned before 11 a.m. Nothing new. I said to sit tight, I was coming out to see him.

The cops were having no luck. It didn't look good. They were going to try to contact Norbert Wyss, Frank's attorney, to see if he might know where Frank was. Earl picked up the phone. He said he was going to call Hagler. He felt he'd better make an excuse for missing the hit, or they might really be tipped off. He'd already been by Hagler's house and his store. The Mark V Continental Bob always drove was not around—anywhere.

One of the workers at Poor Boy's Furniture store answered Earl's call. Earl asked for Bob. He wasn't in. Earl left a message. He said to tell Bob he had to see Frank, right away. The worker told Earl that Frank was supposed to call in just a few minutes. He said to call back.

Earl and I headed for the nearby restaurant where Monday's meeting had taken place. We thought if they could get to Frank, we could call him to the restaurant right away. But when Earl called back, Bob answered. He said Frank was due at his furniture store at 2 p.m. Earl said he'd be there to meet him. He eased the phone back into the cradle.

I fished for a dime and called Foote.

"If you want Frank, he's going to be at 2310 S. Calhoun at 2 p.m.," I said. "I'll be in the vicinity."

"All right," Foote said. "Don't drive your own car, that's all. And tell Earl to stay away."

When I got back to the office it was after noon. I borrowed a late model Chevy Malibu and Dorsett grabbed his cameras. We headed for the meeting site an hour early. We weren't going to be spotted this time. And we wanted a good vantage point to see the action come down. This was it.

We scouted the area twice and found a place in a parking lot next to Ridgeway Auto Parts. We pulled in, flipped on the tape player, and settled back to watch the store front. People were coming and going. No sign of Frank. We saw the county police undercover cars arrive one by one. They took up strategic places. They had this game plan down pat. They were ready. There was nothing left to do but wait.

At 1:37 p.m. Frank Whiting, his wife in the blue Pontiac convertible beside him, pulled down Calhoun Street to the front of Bob Hagler's store. He parked the car. In seconds, the cops were on him.

I rammed the car out of the lot and out onto Calhoun Street. Dorsett jumped from the car, shooting on the move with his long lens. I moved across the street as Foote and Working went inside to nab Hagler. It was a piece of cake. It went as smooth as machinery. It was over in minutes. Frank Whiting looked bewildered. Hagler calmly went on eating from a plastic cup of chili.

Dorsett's film had broken during the frantic shooting, but nothing was damaged. The pictures came out as planned. I headed for the County Courthouse. Two detectives were walking Frank across the marble floor as I came in. He gave me a sidelong, angry look. He was not a happy man. His whole, ragged world had collapsed beneath him. He was asking for his attorney.

Foote was sitting in the sheriff's office. He had a few details to unload. Frank's age? 48. Hagler? 40. Frank's address? Not known. The charge? Conspiracy to commit murder. $50,000 bond. The case? Very tight. I called Earl.

"It's all over," I said.

He already knew. He'd watched the whole thing go down from across the street.

There were a few loose pieces to tie down. I wanted to see Parker Whiting. I had to see his face, to know him as something besides just a name. Dorsett went out to the Health Center with me. The sun was starting to sink in the west. There were a few high, blue, cirrus clouds.

Parker and his wife, Betty, were in the director's office. Tom Kasantis, the director, was with them, explaining the situation to Parker, trying, in some way, to let him know as gently as human kind could do, that his own son had plotted his murder. A death sentence. Death by suffocation.

When I went in Parker was sitting beside the Reb. Kleinschmidt. Betty had her hand against his arm. He was sitting in his wheelchair with his blue robe on, wearing pajamas like most days. His aged face was red, and his clear, blue eyes were filled with tears. Every time Frank's name was mentioned, he began to cry again.

We talked quietly. I asked a couple of questions about Frank. Betty Whiting said he stopped working with Parker's company some 18 years ago. He'd been self-employed. I asked what he'd been doing the last few years.

"What has he been doing the last few years?" Betty said. She shook her head. The question was an echo, and an answer.

I asked about the racing stable of trotters and pacers that Parker used to own. About the stockyards where Whiting's daily hog reports were read for years over the local radio stations. About little things. It was no time to talk of the crime. There was enough sadness there.

When we left Parker and Betty, Tom Kasantis took us down to Parker's room and showed us his bed. He described Parker as an alert and cheerful man. He said they often had pleasant conversations in the hall outside Parker's room. Then he took us down to the privacy room. The room where Frank Whiting planned to have his father killed. Someone had moved the towels that Frank had left there for the purpose. Tom pointed out where they had been.

Dorsett and I walked out of the Health Center and out onto the asphalt parking lot where we had been scared off four days before. The sun was going down over a stand of trees far to the west. It was glowing bright orange and the color seemed to drip from the clouds strung out like cotton across the sky. I started thinking about what Frank had said—about how his father liked to sit and look out the window. Dorsett must have been reading my mind.

"It'd been a shame for Parker to miss a sunset like this, wouldn't it?" he said.

That seemed to sum it all up.

Judge Shows Mercy on Defendants

A former Huntertown man who tried to have his elderly father murdered two years ago was to come before Noble Circuit Court Judge Robert Probst late this morning to close the book on this city's most publicized murder conspiracy.

Frank Whiting, now of Sturgis, Mich., pleaded guilty to conspiracy to commit murder, was given a suspended sentence, five years' probation and ordered to stay out of Allen County.

Whiting's alleged co-conspirator, Robert Hagler, 40, 1832 S. Webster St., will also plead guilty with recommendation for a suspended sentence and five years' probation, according to Prosecutor Arnold Duemling. Hagler will not be asked to leave town.

Duemling said Monday he recommended the suspended sentences for both men because he believed Frank Whiting plotted a "mercy killing," not a profit-motivated murder.

"Frank's (Whiting's) story—and his brother (Tom Whiting) agrees—is that this was a case of euthanasia," Duemling said. "Tom told us Frank wouldn't have come into any money by Parker's death, because the estate was in trust."

Parker Whiting, 83, a resident of Byron Health Center, once a prominent and wealthy businessman in Fort Wayne, was to be suffocated in a sun room at the nursing home December 17, 1979.

Earl Harts, a local scrap dealer, turned down an offer of $5,000 to murder Parker Whiting with a pillow, and instead, turned over information to police who arrested Whiting and Hagler on December 18, 1979.

Whiting pleaded innocent by reason of insanity in January 1981, after the case had already been before the court for more than a year.

Hagler pleaded innocent in March 1980, but his case was continued two years by agreement with Duemling, in exchange for testimony against Whiting when the case came to trial.

Sources close to the case said Hagler had grown more reluctant to testify in the past few months, claiming he did not remember details of the conspiracy because of intoxication. The plea bargain that produced Whiting's guilty plea this morning, however, ended the need for Hagler's testimony.

Duemling said Hagler will enter his plea as soon as an agreement is reached with Hagler's attorney for a court appearance. Hagler could receive a 30-year suspended sentence, sources said.

Duemling said he agreed to a suspended sentence and probation based on discussions with Tom Whiting, who told him Frank Whiting knew at the time of the conspiracy that he wouldn't benefit financially by his father's death.

Whiting told Harts, however, in a meeting that Harts recorded on tape, that he (Whiting) would come into a large sum of money by his father's death.

Whiting, who had been experiencing financial difficulties, was only able to give Harts $8 gasoline money as a down payment, as Harts met Whiting in a meeting that county police kept under surveillance outside.

Ton Katsanis, director of the Byron Health Center where Parker Whiting lives, said yesterday the elder Whiting's condition has remained "virtually unchanged" in the past two years.

"His health isn't good, but he is cheerful and alert. He talks to everyone. I stop by and have a chat now and then myself. I enjoy talking with him," Katsanis said.

When told the plot to kill Whiting was termed euthanasia, Katsanis responded, "ridiculous."

Katsanis said no one from the prosecutor's office has interviewed the elder Whiting or officials at Byron Health Center about the state of his health since the murder plot was exposed.

Whiting's trial was moved to Noble County from Allen Circuit Court because defense attorneys for Whiting felt pretrial publicity would affect a jury. The conspiracy was first exposed by the News-Sentinel, and defense attorneys argued the newspaper "could be expected to sensationalize" the trial.

Both Whiting and Hagler have been out of jail on $35,000 bond since a few days after they were arrested.

Judge Probst also ordered a pre-sentence investigation with a fine to be levied against Whiting.

Part of the delay in the trial occurred while court-appointed psychiatrists examined Whiting to determine if he was competent to stand trial. Sources said the psychiatrists found Whiting was under extreme stress when the conspiracy occurred and did not believe he was dangerous now.

THE VERNON JORDAN SHOOTING

The nation's attention was focused on the City of Fort Wayne in the wake of the shooting there of civil rights leader Vernon Jordan. As national media surrounded the hospital, the author went into the city's black neighborhoods to find reaction on the streets, and take readers along — HMC.

AFTERMATH OF A SHOOTING: LIFE GOES ON ITS WAY

Outside William's Tap on Hanna Street, which is in the heart of the predominantly black neighborhoods of Fort Wayne's central city, a young man was standing late Thursday night, tapping a cane against his hand.

There were several men standing in front of the barroom. It was hot and muggy on Hanna Street and people had come out into the street where there was at least a little breeze and a little air.

The man tapped the cane against his hand and he talked to the other men standing there. They were laughing as they were talking. Nearby a couple of people were sitting on a curb watching traffic go by.

Some twenty hours earlier, Vernon E. Jordan Jr., the 44-year-old civil rights leader and president of the National Urban League, had been shot and critically wounded in a hotel parking lot on the city's north side. The rumors of a racial reaction to the shooting came immediately on the heels of the shooting.

Now, late in the evening Thursday, there were people in the streets in the black community, but it was the heat that drove them there, not unbridled anger.

Howard, who is a man of the street, had been sitting in the Club Societe' on Pontiac Street about noon Thursday. The front door of the bar was open and a small breeze wafted through. Howard was sitting with a white man at a table and they were having a beer. A copy of a newspaper was on one of the chairs and they were talking.

"I don't see it being a racial thing," Howard said. "They are not going to have a 'thing' here. Everything's pretty calm and it'll stay that way. I don't see there is any trouble here."

He sat in the coolest part of the bar and talked that way, and out on the street the traffic was going by in the bright sunshine and the heat was coming down and everything was going on, despite the shooting, as things normally go on at noon on Pontiac Street.

Across town, across from Parkview Hospital, the children at St. Jude's Catholic School were out in the parking lot for recess. They knew something was up because there was so much traffic outside the hospital. Some drivers had ignored the signs in the school parking lot. The kids worked their way around the cars as they played a game. Under the bright sun, across the street from where Vernon Jordan lay in intensive care, fighting for his life, the children sang a child's song and ran, touching, grabbing hands, playing the way children always play.

The traffic outside Parkview had piled up because of the people who had come to find out what had happened and what was going to happen as an aftermath to the shooting. News people had driven headlong, arrived by plane and moved in, anxious, parking their cars in ragged fashion, double-parking, adding an urgency to the situation which had little to do with the important thing—the saving of a life—that was going on inside the intensive care unit at Parkview Hospital.

The dignitaries began to arrive. Civil rights leaders Rev. Jesse Jackson from Chicago and Benjamin Hooks of the NAACP, and local leaders, black and white, began to file into the hospital. Reporters and those carrying television cameras began to arrive, and they put their cameras up in a large semicircle in front of a north wall in the hospital lobby so the crowds could begin to form.

There were the curious and the media en masse. The press conference became forums of information and statements. There were conflicting reports and conflicting statements. And the speculation that always begins to rise where things are not clear-cut began to show itself.

Statements read to the media sent reporters from national television and newspapers and wire services scurrying to the bank of telephones on the south wall of the lobby. More telephones were installed for reporters to use. From above, on a little balcony over the lobby, the crowd seemed to swarm over itself, surging up tight around the table where each new statement was made.

Little changed during the day. The police found a fresh shell casing and found the place from which the shot was fired that felled Jordan. The surgeons, the heroes of the drama, did their work under the bright lights of the operating theater and then monitored. And the leaders who gathered tried to soothe whatever fears there might be of violence erupting. Few new facts were added. The media began to drift away, to return to respective cities to seek out other stories. Television cameramen went home. In the evening, most of them were gone.

With the sun going down, still hot and muggy on Hannah Street, the people came inside for supper and to watch the television. They watched and saw their town on the national news, heard of the fears of violence and then they went back outside on porches and in yards or down to neighborhood taverns. They did this because it was hot, and near summer, and because nothing, despite what the media said, had happened Thursday that yet changed the way they live.

THE PERILS OF BEING A TRUE DETECTIVE

Last week in the Federal Building on Harrison Street downtown, Don Seaman, an FBI agent out of Washington D.C., was just getting to work as the building opened. He came up the stairs into the long, hollow, dimly lit hallway on the third floor and down to the FBI office, which has a wire grating on the window to keep criminals out.

When he sat down at the telephone at a desk inside, he had something on his mind. He was thinking in an indirect way about the President of the United States and about the black civil rights leaders in this country. Mostly he was thinking about the Justice Department. He was thinking this way because the President had been getting heavy political pressure from the nation's black leaders, and the Justice Department has been getting a lot of heat from the President.

What is causing all this trouble is the fact that, still, there are virtually no leads in the shooting of Vernon Jordan, the president of the National Urban League, who was gunned down two months ago in the parking lot of the Marriott Inn on the north side of this city.

Seaman was one of the men on whom it had all come down last Wednesday morning. He had been told directly what he had to do. He had to go back to Fort Wayne and talk to everyone the FBI already talked to about the shooting of Vernon Jordan. Included among these people were the friends of Martha Coleman. So last Wednesday, Seaman picked up the phone and started to work to catch a criminal.

"If you don't mind, we'd like to get together with you and ask you a few questions as part of the investigation," Seaman said over the phone, which came from the FBI's small office directly into the newsroom of this newspaper. He wanted to meet at night, but he agreed to meet at 10:30 that morning in the FBI office downtown. He was waiting there when another Washington agent unlocked the heavy wooden door.

"The Justice Department has instructed us to re-interview people talked to before—a little more thoroughly," he said as he sat in the chair at the table in the outer office of the greatest detective agency in the world. He had a piece of paper and a pencil and he was making notes.

"I hope you don't mind us asking you these questions?"

"No."

"Have you seen Martha Coleman since the incident?"

"Yes, once."

"Did she talk about whether or not she had met Vernon Jordan before the night of the shooting, or whether she had made a special effort to meet him that night?"

"We didn't talk about it at all."

Seaman made a notation on his piece of paper and put his hand to his tie. The tie was framed against his white shirt, which was beneath a navy-blue blazer. The blazer made him look more like an insurance agent than a great detective. He asked some more questions of a personal nature, of things that he thought might shed light on the investigation in some vague way.

"Do you smoke?" he asked, suddenly.

"Sometimes. Not regularly."

"What brand of cigarettes do you smoke?"

"Whatever is available, usually."

"When you buy cigarettes, what brand do you buy?"

He wrote the answer on the paper.

"Do you own any firearms?"

"No."

"Have you had in your possession any firearms in the last few months?"

"Yes. A .38 caliber pistol."

"What was it, a Colt, a Smith & Wesson?"

"I'm not sure, Smith & Wesson I think."

"Do you still have it?"

"No, I returned it to the person I borrowed it from."

"And when was that?"

"I'm not sure. Around the weekend of May 23rd, I think."

"And who did you return it to?"

"I'd rather not say. I don't know if they have a permit for the weapon and I don't want to get them in any trouble."

"Can you tell us where you were on the evening of the May 28 and the morning of the 29th, the night Vernon Jordan was shot?"

"Not really. I don't remember what I did that evening. I assume I was at home."

"Is there anyone you might have been with that could confirm that?"

"Possibly, I don't really remember."

Seaman wrote a name down on the pad. He asked how to get in touch with the person. He asked more questions. He looked at the other agent sitting at the table and asked if he wanted to know anything additional, besides what he'd already asked. The agent looked down at his own pad of paper and shook his head.

"As a newspaperman, can you think of any questions we haven't asked you that we should?" Seaman asked. He smiled when he said it.

"I don't think so."

"Except the big one, I guess." Seaman said. He leaned forward in his chair a little bit. The other agent did, too. There was a long pause. He asked the question quietly.

"Did you shoot Vernon Jordan?" He stared as he said it, and as he got the answer he expected to get.

Then he picked up his piece of paper and put his pencil into the pocket of his white shirt. It was 11 a.m. In Washington it was noon already and the people who now want to know so badly who shot Vernon Jordan were going out to have their lunch.

Later in the day, Seaman would have to call Washington and tell someone up the line what progress he had made, which was none. This apparently is the way it is, right now, in the business of being the greatest detective agency in the world. It is not a good time to be a G-man, when you don't have a lead or a clue or a thing to go on in the biggest case since Patty Hearst decided to come home.

MARTHA COLEMAN: SHE'S NOT TALKING

It came as a surprise. I'd nearly given up Friday afternoon on my two-day attempt to locate Martha Coleman, the alleged "mystery witness" in the sniper shooting of civil rights leader Vernon E. Jordan Jr.

All the leads had been exhausted. Her attorney, Charles Leonard, had made it clear she was where no one would find her. And I'd talked to everyone I could think of.

Then the phone rang. I was expecting any of a dozen calls, and I was not in the mood to take any of them.

"Dan?" the voice said. "This is Martha Coleman."

I had known her for several months. I just talked to her on Tuesday before the Urban League dinner on Wednesday, and we'd made tentative plans to meet Thursday night for a drink.

The calm, confident, self-assured voice I'd heard then was different now. It was tense, strained, frayed—not the voice I'd become accustomed to.

"I got the 97 messages you left around town to have me call you," she said. A pause. "I had 98 from my attorney saying not to call you, but I told him you were a friend and that I was going to call anyway. He said you talked to him Thursday and were concerned."

"I'm a nervous wreck. Other than that, I'm all right. A little frightened, I guess," Martha said. "I've already asked myself a hundred times all the things you're thinking about. I've been all through it already."

Her voice was tired, resigned, almost a sigh. She had spent a long day and night virtually without sleep after five hours of questions by police in the early hours Thursday. She hadn't been able to sleep since then.

"I'm doing whatever my attorneys are advising me to do. I'm letting them handle the thing in the way they think is best. I'm not going to talk about it. You know I'm not going to say anything now. Not until the attorneys say so," Martha said. "I'm a little scared, I'm under a doctor's care, but I'm all right."

She continued, "I don't have anything to hide. I didn't see a thing out there. I told the police that when I talked to them. I didn't see any vehicle; I didn't see any person out there. I heard the shot, but I didn't know what it was then. I didn't know what a gunshot sounded like. I just saw him fall behind the car. That's all."

There was some more small talk. She said she hadn't liked the pictures of her much in the paper, and she wondered where they'd come from.

"I want to get out, I kind of feel like I'm in prison here. I don't have my own car," she said. Her car had been picked up and stashed Thursday afternoon by an attorney. She said she hadn't made any plans about what to do over the next few days.

"I guess there will be one large press conference when they finally decide to do it," she said. "I'm not looking forward to that very much."

Martha Coleman's story was the one that the national press all wanted, and when Luzadder scooped them, they packed up and headed home. Associated Press moved his column verbatim under his byline across the country. - HMC

Chicago Tribune:

Luzadder wrote an account of the ordeal of a Fort Wayne man, Lyle VanAman, who survived the crash of a small plane in the Bermuda Triangle that claimed the lives of three persons close to him. The story was published in the Fort Wayne News Sentinel on Saturday, and bannered the Chicago Tribune's front page on Sunday morning. Luzadder was traveling in northern Michigan at the time and drove an hour through a blizzard, he said, to find the newsstand in Petoskey that sold the Tribune They had a dozen copies and, so he claimed, he could only afford to buy two. - HMC

FLIGHT TURNS TO DEATH RIDE
IN BERMUDA TRIANGLE

Editor's Note: *On Jan. 6, Lyle VanAman, of Fort Wayne, his cousin, Dr. John Thompson, of Fremont, and two friends, Janet Sorrell, of Fort Wayne, and Linda Dienhart, of Indianapolis, left St. Martin's Island in the Caribbean, aboard a Cessna 210.*

They were in high spirits, ending a 12-day vacation in the islands and heading toward Florida.

Suddenly, with little warning, their plane developed a serious, mysterious problem, forcing pilot Thompson to ditch the plane at sea — in the Bermuda Triangle.

All four survived the crash—shaken, but unhurt. However, one-by-one, three of the four succumbed to exhaustion, exposure and the relentless sea. Miraculously, VanAman survived three days and two nights of 30-foot waves, leech-like creatures, unbearable sun and an agonizing thirst.

News-Sentinel "Street Talk" columnist and reporter Dan Luzadder recently spent many hours with VanAman, tape-recording his recollections of the events leading up to the crash at sea, of his thoughts throughout his 52 hours of drifting aimlessly, and of his conversations with his three friends as each came face to face with death.

It is a gripping story of courage, death and survival.

There had been no warning. The Caribbean Sea was sparkling like crystal beneath the single-engine Cessna 210 aircraft as John Thompson, pilot and retired surgeon, banked and headed north.

The plane had just passed Haiti's northwestern shoreline and was heading into the Bermuda Triangle near Great Inagua Island to refuel. It had been a smooth, uneventful three-hour flight from St. Martin Island. Suddenly, everything changed.

Lyle VanAman, a husky, robust man of 46, was sitting beside his cousin and long-time flying companion as the pilot studied his maps for the approach to the island airfield. In the rear seats Janet Sorrell, 42, and Linda Dienhart, 35, were chatting over the engine noise and reading. Great Inagua had just become visible on the horizon when John sounded the alert.

"Oh-oh," he said. "I think we've got trouble."

John was checking the instrument panel and tapping the tachometer with his knuckles. "The RPMs are way too high," he said. "The prop is slowing."

VanAman looked over the cowling at the propeller. It was pinwheeling. John half-turned in his seat. Smoke trickled into the cockpit.

"Get your seatbelts fastened tight. I think we're going to have to set her down," he told the women. "Make sure your lifejackets are secure."

In those few moments there began an ordeal Lyle VanAman will never forget. What had been a cheerful Caribbean holiday trip was to become a fight for survival against odds too great to calculate.

John reached for the radio. They had just descended from 8,000 feet and were flying at 2,500 feet. Now they were gliding without power, losing altitude quickly. He flipped the switch open and tried to call Great Inagua. There was no answer. He reached up, changed channels, and began repeating "Mayday—Mayday," into the black hand-mike. On the second call a response crackled over the speaker.

"We are crashing at sea," John said. He gave the aircraft's identification numbers. "180 degrees off Great Inagua Island, 20 to 30 miles out."

The pilot of an Eastern Airlines jet, high overhead, repeated the location and began to ask a question. He was cut off in mid-sentence.

"We didn't have time to answer it," VanAman said. "At that moment, we hit the water."

Land disappeared from sight as the small red and black craft skidded into the waves with its landing gear up. It came to an abrupt halt. Water began to seep up through the cockpit floor as John dropped the mike. The impact knocked VanAman's glasses off. They clattered against the windshield and fell into the water at his feet.

"Come on, let's get out of here," John yelled. He slid his seat forward to let Linda out ahead of him. Lyle's hands were trembling as he pulled his seatbelt loose. Jan flipped the door handle and leaped into the water. Lyle followed her out, plunging into the sun-bright water beneath the wing.

"We all went under and when I came up I remember hearing John calling Linda," VanAman said. "He couldn't find her at first. Jan and I couldn't see them, but I remember John yelling to us, asking if Linda got out all right. Just as he said it, he turned and saw her behind him. She was all right, but pretty frightened and having trouble inflating her Mae West. John helped her trip the CO_2 cartridge and it was inflated when they swam around the tail of the plane."

Lyle and Jan had paddled a few feet from the cockpit door and now leaned against the edge of the right wing. The cockpit was filling fast. John tugged at them, trying to keep water out of his mouth as he spoke.

"Get back, away from the plane," he said. "It's going to go down. We don't want to go with it."

They had backed off, perhaps 10 feet, VanAman said, watching the craft settle lower and lower. Then it nosed forward.

"It gave a couple of gurgles and went completely out of sight," he said. "It was just gone. The tail went down last."

Moments before the aircraft disappeared, a carved wooden plaque about three feet long popped out the cabin door. It was one of four souvenirs like it that VanAman and the women had bought two days earlier on St. Martin Island. As it floated toward them, they grasped it and held on. It was the only debris which escaped as the plane sank.

"After the initial fear and surprise, we all calmed down," VanAman said. "It happened so fast we were in the water before we had time to think about it. There was a lot of fear but no panic. We had called in the Mayday and heard it acknowledged. We'd seen land before the crash. We were sure there would be boats out from the island. It was only 3 p.m.

"Great Inagua was the only place to refuel in the area so we expected other aircraft to be flying over us. We were sure a general alert had been given so other pilots would be looking for us in the area. We simply had all the confidence in the world we'd be picked up quickly. We thought it might be an hour or two at the most. The plane was lost, but we were unhurt. I don't think it crossed our minds what might happen."

Jan and Lyle were wearing zippered, foam-flotation lifejackets, which Lyle had bought in a discount store before the trip. The jackets kept their heads and tops of their shoulders out of the water. John and Linda's lifejackets caused them to ride lower in the sea. They all clung to the wooden plaque. The two-to-three-foot waves caused them to bob up and down as they talked, even laughed.

"We were still frightened, of course," VanAman said. "But there was no panic. Everything was as good as could be expected. I had apparently bumped my leg pretty hard in the crash but I didn't even realize it at the time."

"We talked about being rescued and the girls asked John how long he thought it would take. He was optimistic and told them so. We even joked about it. Jan had read a story earlier about the Bermuda Triangle in a magazine and we talked about that. None of us had ever taken it seriously."

As the first hour wore on, the four began to get accustomed to being afloat in the ocean. The salt water stung their eyes and lips. When a wave broke near them, spraying in their faces, the water made them cough and gag. It was mild at first, but was to get worse.

Hours in Sea Harsher Than Crash
Fish, Waves Plague Victims

Editor's Note: *Lyle VanAman and Janet Sorrell, of Fort Wayne, Dr. John Thompson, of Fremont, and Linda Dienhart, of Indianapolis, all escaped shaken, but unhurt, from their crash at sea.*

However, the crash itself was to seem minor compared to what they were about to endure, alone and adrift at sea.

Following is the second of five articles in which VanAman, the sole survivor of that trauma, recounts the agony of that first night.)

"When we spit salt water out it burned a lot," VanAman said. "You had to be kind of careful how you breathed so you didn't get water in your lungs. Later we couldn't help it—when the seas started really getting rough."

They had been in the water for more than two hours when the sun began to go down across the horizon. They had scanned the sky constantly but had not seen a single aircraft or ship.

"We thought it was kind of unusual because we expected more air traffic. But we didn't see a thing. We started talking a lot about survival and what to do if no one came before dark. Gradually we realized we weren't going to be rescued that day. Being out there in the water at night scared us, but there wasn't much we could do about it. We began to pray. We prayed out loud for a while and I think we were praying to ourselves continuously at first. I'd hear the others mumbling sometimes and I assumed they were praying. We said the Lord's Prayer together. And we asked for help."

Darkness settled over the ocean and the seas began to rise silently. Though they could not see land, they knew they were drifting away from the site where the plane went down. They didn't know how fast or how far.

As night closed in, the skies became overcast. Sometime during the night, it rained. Lyle let the water trickle into his mouth. The seas became nearly placid during the shower and when the rain stopped the moon came out, lighting up the water around them. Lyle looked at his watch. It was about 10 p.m. when they sighted the first ship.

"We were still clinging to the plaque to keep us together. One of us, I can't remember who, saw a ship about a mile away. It was a schooner-type vessel. The moonlight on the water was bright and we could see clearly enough to tell it's sails were down. It was apparently running by engine, but we couldn't hear it. It moved silently past us. We began to shout and holler at it, but there was no response. We yelled until we didn't have the strength to yell anymore."

In the saltwater waves they had encountered a new problem—the struggle to keep their feet down so their heads would not dip backward and allow water to wash over their faces. It meant they had to keep their feet moving constantly in a dog-paddle-like motion. The movement was tiring. The water that did wash over them stirred searing pain inside their noses. About midnight they spotted something moving on the horizon.

"There were what appeared to be two cruise ships, big ones," VanAman said. "We could see the rows of lights on different decks. One passed a little while before the other, both going in the same direction. We tried yelling again. But it wasn't any use."

The night wore slowly on. There was no sleeping. They held tightly to the plaque, talking to stay calm. Sometime during the night, they began to talk about what had happened to the plane.

"John was a surgeon, not a mechanic, but he knew the plane pretty well. He said he thought the crankshaft may have snapped, but he didn't know for sure. He felt it had to be something like that for the engine to start running fast and the prop to quit. I couldn't remember hearing the engine race. I only knew something was wrong when John told us."

Several times in the water John mentioned the irony of their situation. The strapping, six-foot tall, 60-year-old adventuresome pilot said he thought it was "just bad luck."

"If it had been 10 minutes earlier when it happened," VanAman said, "we'd have been over the coast of Haiti and could have set down on the beach. If it had been 10 minutes later, we would have been over Great Inagua and would probably have made the airport. But we didn't have that extra 10 minutes either way."

The U.S. Coast Guard had been alerted that Thompson's plane was down off Great Inagua within minutes after his Mayday call and had sent fixed-wing aircraft to search for them in the hours before darkness. They made sweeps of the crash site several times, but spotted nothing. They looked for debris from the crash, but found none. Apparently, John's skillful landing had worked against them. At dark, the search planes returned to land.

"Sometime during the night, not too long after dark, a fish swam near us at the surface. It looked to be dark, about three-foot long and about as big around as your calf muscle. It swam right up next to us," VanAman said. "I took the plaque and took two swings at it, hitting it on the side, I think. We didn't see it again, but it made us think about sharks and we talked about them. Because we didn't see any, we decided there weren't any in the area."

When the rain stopped, VanAman said he noticed luminous-looking objects in the water near them.

"They seemed to be some kind of shellfish," he said. "We tried to brush them away, but they were all around us on the surface and started attaching themselves to our skin. It felt like a mosquito bite. They got beneath our clothes, which made it worse. We'd pinch them off with our fingers. It didn't hurt badly, but it annoyed the hell out of us."

The four survivors were eagerly awaiting dawn and they scanned the skies for the first signs of light. But with the dawn came more problems. The seas began to worsen. The waves climbed from two feet to four, then to six.

VanAman was no stranger to bad weather. As a troubleshooter for Indiana & Michigan Electric Company, he was accustomed to working in freezing temperatures, sleet, snow, rain and in other hazardous conditions. He had been shocked and had fallen from poles, but was never seriously hurt. As one of the first electricians called to a scene, he had worked against impossible conditions. But what he was about to encounter was unlike anything he had experienced before.

Hallucinations, Death Claims 2 As Crash Victims Not Found

Editor's Note: After a sleepless night adrift at sea, plane crash victims Lyle VanAman and Janet Sorrell, of Fort Wayne, Dr. John Thompson of Fremont, and Linda Dienhart of Indianapolis, looked forward to the light of the day. To them it meant increased odds for being seen and rescued "any minute." But the "minutes" dragged into hours. Following is the third of five articles in which VanAman, the sole survivor of that crash, recounts how two of his three companions succumbed to the sea, leaving just two of them to face another cold, frightening night.

Lyle remembered feeling relieved to have made it through the night. Everyone was all right, but fatigue was creeping up on them. No one had slept because no one knew how, and they were afraid to try.

With first light, and despite the waves, they felt better. Daylight meant new searches. Slowly they were learning to cope with the waves.

At first, they were dunked with each passing swell, gagging and choking on the salt water. Then they forced themselves to inhale, hold their breath, then exhale when water broke over them.

"I remember it being hard to see because I'd lost my glasses in the crash," VanAman said. "But we began to see objects in the distance. We thought we saw more ships, but they were quite a ways off. The waves were giving us a lot of trouble and we were looking for signs of aircraft. We still didn't see any. I kept checking my watch, which was still running."

"By the time nine o'clock rolled around, John said we ought to be seeing someone any minute."

Those minutes became hours. The sun grew hot. Their parched lips began to blister.

"By noon, we still hadn't seen anyone. Early in the afternoon, a ship came in sight about a mile distant. It passed directly in front of us, made a right turn, came to our right, and made another right turn. Then they pulled about even with us, and turned left—away from us."

Linda had taken off her bright colored blouse she had worn over a T-shirt and tied it to the plaque. Lyle began to wave it as high over his head as he could, back and forth. But it was no use.

"My arms got so tired I couldn't hold it up anymore. My feet kept coming up and I'd get dunked. John tried it, but they didn't see us. If they hadn't made that left turn, it looked like they would have come right by us."

By now they had been in the water 20 hours. They had seen four ships, and, as each one passed them by, they grew more and more discouraged. Finally, they decided they must try to help themselves. A few minutes later they spotted what they thought was a marker buoy. John tied the plaque to his belt with Linda's blouse and they began to swim in the growing seas.

The waves had surged to 15 feet and higher. They tried swimming together but could not make headway. Jan and Lyle began to body surf on the crest of the waves. Slowly, John and Linda fell behind. They were afraid of getting separated. At one point they were apart by 60 feet. They treaded water while John and Linda caught up. At the top of a wave they thought they saw land again, but it was apparently a mirage. The marker buoy turned out to be the same. It, too, had "disappeared."

At last, they gave up swimming. For every stroke of progress, they seemed to lose two. The exertion had taken its toll. When John and Linda caught up the last time, John was exhausted. His Mae West had developed a leak. Every 20 minutes he had to blow it up again with a valve on the side. The fatigue and fear were beginning to show on his face. He asked Lyle if he could hold to his lifejacket.

"It was getting late in the day and we could tell John was having a rough time of it. We tried to get him to relax. I held on to him and Jan floated flat in the water, when she could, so that John could rest his head against her. But the waves were too bad. He kept saying he hoped they would find us soon or that we would find something to crawl up on before nightfall. After a while, John pulled himself closer to me."

"I'm not going to make it," he told Lyle. "I don't think I can hold out. If I don't, I want you to take my wallet and give it to my mother. Take the money belt. If you get out of this, spend it."

"He continued to hold to my lifejacket for a while," VanAman said. "But gradually he leaned farther back in the water. He stopped blowing saltwater out.

"I was holding him up, trying to talk to him, but he didn't answer.

"I shook him, but he didn't respond. I held him up for a long time. Finally, Linda, who was a nurse, paddled to me."

"I don't think you need to hold him any longer," she said. "He's gone."

"Still," VanAman said, "I couldn't bring myself to let him go. I guess I held on for another 10 minutes or so. Then I took his wallet and I put his money belt on Jan. I took his Mae West and put it on Linda. I don't know if he died of drowning, exposure or exhaustion or of all three. But I finally realized he was gone."

It was early in the evening of the second day. Lyle, Jan and Linda clung together. The plaque had been lost in the tiring swim so they held to each other. The seas had grown very heavy. VanAman described the waves as 30 feet high.

Again and again as they were lifted they thought they saw land. But there were other hallucinations. They became afraid to trust their own senses.

"It was about two hours after John died, and darkness was coming on," VanAman recalled. "Linda began to get a lot of energy. She swam a little ways off from Jan and me and started splashing around like she was in a big swimming pool. She was laughing and talking to people who she knew at the hospital where she worked, having a good time. We tried to get her to calm down, but she didn't hear us. I guess she was out of her head. Then she got behind us. About five minutes later when we looked around, she was face down in the water. She was dead."

Linda's death had shocked Lyle and Jan. She had seemed calm when John died. She had complained of being cold earlier and was afraid of being colder, after losing her blouse, if they had to go through another night. It had grown dark and the two survivors knew they faced another long night in the chilly sea together.

The Lone Survivor

"Jan and I took the *Mae West* (life jacket) Linda was wearing and we each put one on. We figured they couldn't help Linda any longer and they might help us."

"We were pretty tired by that time. I had been struggling to keep my pants on, but finally I lost them. The cuffs were rolled up around my legs and the top had come loose in the water."

"I began to wonder what else the saltwater would do, especially to the lifejackets. I worried that it would eat through the lining and they would fall apart. We had been hoping against hope that an aircraft would spot us before dark, or that maybe we'd even make land. Neither of us thought we could make it through another night."

"I had said earlier, when we all were talking, that I would hold out just as long as I possibly could, to the very last bit of strength I had. But we had worn ourselves out swimming and both Jan and I were exhausted. The waves battered us and made it hard to breathe. Our skin was sunburned."

"The waves were so high that at one point when you were in the trough it looked like you were looking up from the basement through the top of a two-story house. The salt kept getting more painful. That wore us down, too."

It was dark and the moon had risen, spreading light across the water, making it like day. Jan and Lyle talked, about what he could not remember. He could remember clearly the fatigue and the tiny leech-like shellfish that returned at night. There were more hallucinations, as they saw at one time what looked like an off-shore oil-drilling rig. Once, Lyle thought he saw high voltage power lines rising up from the sea.

Now, alone, they held to each other. The seas had calmed somewhat and in their exhaustion Jan and Lyle spoke only briefly.

The hours wore on. About midnight, for the first time since they crashed into the sea, Lyle fell asleep. It was a brief nap, no longer, he thought, than a few minutes. But after that, sleep came easier. They had been without water for more than 35 hours and they prayed often that rain would fall so they could at least get a little water into their mouths.

Jan, too, dozed briefly. They began to drift in and out of sleep. Each time Lyle awakened he asked Jan if she was all right. Each time she replied she was "doing okay."

Lyle kept a firm grip on her lifejacket. They held each other closely.

"Sometime before dawn the moon went down and it became very dark," VanAman said. "It was during that time that I awoke from a short sleep and called out to Jan. She didn't answer. I shook her in the dark, thinking she was asleep. I slapped her lightly on the cheeks to try to wake her but she didn't respond."

"I began to be afraid she was dying. I tried to give her mouth-to-mouth resuscitation. But in the waves, it was very hard and I was very tired. Finally, just before dawn, I realized she was dead."

"I remember her speaking to John early in the morning of the second day, him being a surgeon, asking if drowning was an easy death. I recalled him saying that it was probably easier than most, but that it took a little time."

"When I was asleep, holding on to Jan, I dreamed that she and I had managed to swim up to a large, U-shaped pier and that there was a big, white ship tied up there at a dock. We had been so happy and cried over having found it and being saved. As I floated there, thinking about Jan being dead, it just seemed to me somehow that that ship had taken her. It was just how I felt about it, that it was a beautiful way to go."

Jan's death, Lyle said, filled him with a great and overwhelming sadness. They had talked many times of their future, had been friends for nine years and had spent many happy times together. They had talked of marriage. John's death, too, had left a deep scar of sadness and pity inside him. But now he began to feel the sudden and total aloneness. He began to think about dying, as if to wish for death himself.

"I was alone. I knew that. I don't know if I was frightened. I figured I was next. I had lost my good friends one by one. I wondered over and over again why we didn't just die in the crash if we were all going to have to die anyway. It seemed so senseless. Then I decided that our times were just not up together, not all at the same time. That it had to be this way. I thought about what it would be like to die and wondered why I didn't just give up. I thought about sticking my head down in the water. I even drank in some of the saltwater. But I spit it right back up. I knew right then I would hang on until I couldn't last any longer."

On Dec. 5, 1945, shortly after the end of World War II, five Grumman TBM Avenger torpedo bombers took off from the U.S. Naval Air Station at Fort Lauderdale, Fla., on a routine training flight.

They were never heard from again.

Nor was any debris or wreckage of the five planes ever found. And the 14 crewmen (three aboard each of four TBMs, two aboard the other) disappeared without a trace.

Equally mystifying, a twin-engine Martin PBM patrol bomber with a crew of 13 aboard, was dispatched in search of the lost flight. The PBM never was heard from again.

Since then, more than 100 planes and ships and more than 1,000 persons have disappeared in the "Bermuda Triangle," an area bounded roughly by Florida, Puerto Rico and Bermuda.

Actually, while the world's attention began to focus on the "Bermuda Triangle" after the 1945 disappearance of the six navy planes, vessels and people had been reported disappearing in the area since the previous century.

In January, 1880, for example, the British frigate Atalanta, with 290 aboard, vanished shortly after leaving Bermuda for England. And in March, 1918, the 500-foot U.S. Navy supply ship USS Cyclops, with 309 aboard, disappeared without a trace en route from Barbados to Norfolk. At first, she was deemed the victim of a German submarine, but a postwar check ruled this out.

A host of theories—some more bizarre than the "Bermuda Triangle" mystery itself—have been proffered in explanation.

Depending on whom you believe, everything from UFO activity, to the moon's influence, to a "time-space warp" accounts for the strange happenings in the triangle.

In the hours that followed Janet's death, Lyle slipped into a semi-conscious state. It was his third day in the water. He felt as though he was in a daze.

Now he remembers only reciting numbers over and over again in his head, as though it was some kind of game he was forced to play. If the numbers totaled a certain amount, without going over a certain figure, it meant, he said, that something would happen. What it was, he does not know.

"I think I lost the whole last day," he said. "I don't remember seeing or hearing anything. The Navy rescue plane that spotted me said I waved to them. But I don't remember it."

Ironically, it was the crash of another light plane that saved VanAman. The Navy search team that found him came across debris from another aircraft about 30 miles off the coast of Cuba. It was the third day of searching without seeing anything. When they saw the debris, they followed it. Then they saw a body, later identified as John's. Then they saw VanAman. Jan and Linda's bodies were never found.

It was nearly five o'clock when the Coast Guard helicopter on standby at Grand Turk Island found VanAman. They swooped low to be sure he was alive, then turned and came back.

"It was the first thing I remember seeing the helicopter going over. I thought, 'Oh God, please let them see me.' In less than a few seconds they were hovering overhead. The man running the bosun's chair put it down inches away from me. They told me later I leaped into it before it hit the water. All I know is that I had never seen anything so beautiful or felt anything like that feeling before in my life."

The search and rescue mission had begun more than 50 hours before when the Eastern Airlines pilot who heard John Thompson's Mayday related the message to the Coast Guard Operations Center in Miami, Fla. A fixed-wing aircraft had been dispatched to search the area, but was forced back by darkness the first night. They resumed their search at dawn the next day, joined by a Navy plane from Guantanamo Bay Naval Base in Cuba. The crews searched without success until dark the second day. It was mid-afternoon of the third day when the aircraft crewmen spotted VanAman. He appeared, they said, to be waving. One of the crewmen began dropping flares and smoke devices. In his excitement, he threw his sack lunch out into the sea.

The rescuers also sighted dolphins swimming near VanAman. They later told him that perhaps it may have been the dolphins—natural enemies of sharks—that saved him from shark attacks. No one knows how long the dolphins might have been near him.

In the helicopter, they gently eased VanAman from the lift chair and onto a bench seat. They wrapped him in a shock blanket and began to ask about other survivors. He told them he was the only one left alive. The co-pilot came back to question further before ordering the helicopter back to Guantanamo Naval Hospital.

VanAman asked for water and the nurse on board gave him sections of an orange. The fruit stung his salt-saturated mouth and throat, but he sucked it down. He asked for more, each time requesting more when it was gone.

"When we landed at the base, they had an ambulance waiting. They put me on a stretcher outside the helicopter and took me inside. They gave me gauze bandages dipped in water to suck on. But I couldn't get enough. They kept it up for hours while they examined me. Oddly enough, my blood pressure, which had been high for years, was normal. My legs and feet were badly swollen and I was badly burned. I couldn't stand for anything to touch my mouth or lips. The doctors told me that my size had probably saved me, the fat insulating me from the elements. I don't know what it was. I only knew I couldn't give up."

For five days, VanAman was kept in a hospital bed, eventually taken off intravenous feedings. The second day he was given some soft foods. The fourth day he tasted solid food again.

Crewmembers of the search plane came to visit him in the hospital. The commander of the unit, Capt. William Edward Zidbeck, told him it was the crew's 40th rescue mission—and the first one in which they found anyone alive.

"I guess that made me kind of a celebrity to the crew," he said.

"Someone told me later the rate of survival for persons down in the Bermuda Triangle was around two percent. That isn't very many. I understand now why they were so surprised to find me alive."

In all, VanAman had drifted some 45 miles from the place where the aircraft went down that Saturday afternoon, January 6. It was a long way from his home in Fort Wayne, Indiana. He was off the coast of Cuba when he was found. And he believes he was near death.

"I'm sure I wouldn't have made it through another night," he said. "If they hadn't found me when they did, I think I would have joined the others."

Most air-sea rescue searches are called off after 72 hours. Navy personnel said despite the mild water temperature of the area, a body cannot survive, usually, nearly that long. VanAman made it through more than 52 hours. Probably, he said, because he refused to die.

"I'm alive. I don't know how to answer when people ask me why. That's all up to the good Lord. Only He can answer that one."

Part 3

Life in the City: Everyday People

Fort Wayne is an historic city; it's origins and relationship to water-borne commerce, before there were land-based alternatives to shipping, changed the face of the region and dictated its place within the cultural realm. Where native Americans once lived and loved, raised children, grew crops, traded and told stories, the westward migration changed everything but the rivers.

The city was changing again in the early 1980s, and not all of that evolution would leave it ready to embrace a changing world. Yet in that era, and into the present, its character would retain all but its outward trappings. Luzadder captured the city's mood, it's place and its practices in his columns, which were sometimes no more than a record of sights and sounds. But those techniques, he learned, could often say more than facts and circumstance. Sometimes he blended both. His first "column" - stopping by a fire next to a church on a Sunday morning, while taking a ride on his bike - was not a column at all, but a news story. Yet the writing would inspire the paper's editor to end the author's tenure on the copy desk, and instead give him a regular column that would endure, thrice a week, for seven years, totaling some 900 in all. - HMC

AND THE FAITHFUL PRAYED ON

By the time the last explosion hit Allen County Tires late Sunday morning, the faith of the parishioners at Emmaus Lutheran Church next door had been well established.

Though the major fire billowed heavy smoke, and the flames turned half the block into a hell-like inferno, the Rev. Carl Schlutz kept his congregation in the fold.

"There was a lot of noise, and I'm sure some people were uneasy. We kept assuring them that if the danger became too great, we would be notified. But we stayed and worshipped."

Rev. Schlutz heard some muffled sounds which were probably the explosions hurling fireballs at firefighters battling through unbearable heat inside the tire store. Later, he said, there was a rumbling that shook the area when the roof and walls of the structure began to collapse.

"About 11 a.m. the lights went out and the organ stopped playing," Rev. Schlutz said. "That caused some concern, but no one panicked. We assured them it was to be expected."

Fortunately for the parish, the wind mercifully blew from the south, carrying the thick smoke from the burning rubber away from the church. But the fire was adjacent to the church's youth classrooms, a mere 30 feet away, and the heat filled the classrooms until the windows cracked. A few feet away the services went on.

As the heat grew, firefighters poured water onto the side of the church. "The sound of the rushing water against the brick startled a good many people. 'We are not on fire,' I told them. It is just a precaution," Rev. Schlutz said.

People shifted in their pews, but they did not leave. When the parish's new Vicar Alan Goebbert found his organ music stilled by the power failure, Rev. Schlutz said all singing stopped.

"We didn't continue a cappella. I told the congregation that the wires had just probably burned through, cutting the power. At that point I'm not sure we would have been able to hit the right pitch, anyway."

Smoke seeped into the church when doors in the youth classroom were opened to release building heat.

"You could smell it quite clearly, even though the wind was blowing away from us," Rev. Schlutz said. "We were ever-conscious of the fire. Proper emergency exits were pointed out before the service began."

The sermon, which Rev. Schlutz said concerned "the peace and comfort one receives from worshipping in the house of the Lord," was not cut short. Other parts of the service were eliminated and the service ended about 10 minutes early, at 11:20 a.m.

One small disappointment, Rev. Schlutz said, "was that there were more people outside the church than inside."

According to reports, smoke from the fire caused temporary evacuation of the Plymouth Congregational Church at 501 West Berry St.

Officials said today, however, that a routine fire drill had been conducted at the church at the same time, and was not related to the heavy smoke. The drill had been planned for two weeks.

WIDOW OF VIOLENCE WOULD TURN JUDGMENT OVER TO GOD

Down on the corner of Lewis and Hanna there was a man sitting in the side doorway of Atkins Package Store with a bottle in a sack. In the rear, in the parking lot, a small cluster of men stood around a trash barrel and some parked cars, across an empty lot from Spiritual Israel Church. It was about 10:30 a.m. and the air was chilly, filled with the threat of rain.

Charline Mims was in her front room a few blocks down on Lewis. When she went back to sit down at the dining room table she left the front door open so that only the screen door was closed. The gray morning light poured in across the couch and coffee table and spilled in the curtained window behind her.

"I've told the detectives," she said. "There isn't much else to say about it. I don't know what good telling more people about the whole thing is doing to do." She was leaning back in her chair and her brown eyes were cloudy, stormy.

She reached for a cigarette pack lying on the plastic table cloth and offered one. She tapped the cigarette end on the table for a long time before she spoke.

A little over two months ago, Charline came home from a long hospital stay to find her husband, the Rev. Charles Mims, slumped over in a chair in the front room of his apartment. The paper said there was a pool of blood at his feet. Sometime during the night, someone had come in the door with a .38 while Charles sat drinking a beer. He never saw them, because he was blind. The person with the gun held it close to Charles' face and pulled the trigger five times. That's all it took. He died where he sat. A strange closing to a strange life.

"You tell me what good it will do if those detectives ever find out who did this thing," Charline said. "They put him or her in prison and what happens when they come out. Which are they gonna be, a punk, a drug addict, or a prostitute? What good's it gonna do for that? You think 12 people can sit downtown in a courtroom and judge that person? God's gonna do the judging. There's no escaping that judgment day. Let God be the judge of it all, just like it says right there in the Bible. Judge not and be ye' not judged. That's what I believe."

Charles Mims was a minister, a big man, strong and self-confident, Charline said. He was also no stranger to violence. About 18 years ago, in Cleveland, Mississippi, he had gone after a man in anger. The man had a shotgun and pulled the trigger as Charles tried to come in through the screen door. The blast hit Charles in the face. He was 27 years old then and the doctors decided he was going to die. They cleaned the wounds but they didn't bother to take the pellets out of his head. They just closed him up and left him blind.

"He fooled 'em," Charline said. "He lived. But it was those pellets that made him sick. He'd get bad every once in a while, you know, confused. He'd start to drinking. Then it would go away and he'd be himself again. He was a good man. The best man I ever knew. But when the Devil got ahold of him, it was bad. Real bad."

Charline's granddaughter was playing in the next room and she came out and crawled up on a chair. She flashed a big, bright smile. Her hair was braided tight on top of her head. She threw a sock onto the table and Charline made her get down and go out of the room.

"Charles and I were together 12 years this December," she said. "When we came up to Fort Wayne, about 1972, he had decided he wanted to preach. That's when we started in with the Spiritual Israel Church. He'd preach every other Sunday and every other Wednesday. We both worked with Lutheran Outreach. Very few people knew Charles was blind. He wouldn't let anybody talk about his handicap in front of him. He'd walk down the street without a stick or anything, he'd come up to something and he'd walk right around it, just like he could see. He had a very special gift. He didn't take any pity, and he didn't expect anyone else to either."

"I'll tell you this about him. Some people say our life together was a hard one. But it was full of experience. That's the way Charles had to be. He cared about people. He wanted to know what it felt like to have to sleep in a vacant building and be a bum. So, he tried it. He felt compassion. I used to tell him not to open up the door to strangers, or let people in the house that he didn't know. But he wouldn't listen. He taught me a lot of things. He made me a different person. I don't even believe he is gone now. He's still right here inside, aiding me along.

"I remember one time we were walking down the street together and we came on another blind man who was sitting on the curb beggin'. Charles sat down beside him and he started talkin' to him. He told him to get up on his own feet and stop beggin' and go out and find him a job. He wouldn't tolerate giving up.

"I'm not saying he was any saint. He had his bad spells. He'll have to answer for that. But he had the love of the Lord in him and he shared it.

He trusted people when he knew they'd do him wrong. That's the way he was. And there never was a harder workin' man. He did all the housework around here. He'd mop the floors, do the washing. He was strong that way. He gave me strength, too.

"When I came home from the hospital that day and found him, it was some of that strength that kept me going. I had been very sick and was still very weak. But the Lord shielded me. I shed very few tears. I still haven't cried very much. That's because my strength is in the Lord."

On Sunday afternoon, May 27, Charline will present a completed nursery to the congregation at the Spiritual Israel Church in memory of Rev. Charles Mims. She took her savings and bought carpet, paneling, paint and nursery characters to put on the walls. With the nursery for the young children, there will be less disruption in the services in the big hall on East Douglas Street where the congregation meets.

"It's something that Charles would have liked," she said. "It's just a small memorial. But when you can take bad and do something good out of it, I think that is what...I just think that would have pleased him."

STANLEY JOINER'S LIFE IN TROUBLED WORLD ENDED VIOLENTLY

For a long way down south Fairfield Avenue early Friday night the red and white lights of the ambulance flickered. Some kind of trouble.

From a few blocks away you could see the ambulance sitting on the edge of the sidewalk in front of Southwood Park Liquors. The shape of a police car swam out of the darkness. A small crowd had gathered.

Minutes earlier Stanley Joiner, 522 Lewis St., a 19-year-old high school dropout who had been laid off eight weeks ago from Superior Iron and Metal, walked in the front door. In his pocket the cold, heavy metal of a small, steel-blue revolver made a weighted feel. In a life filled with bad decisions, Stanley Joiner was about to make his last.

If you've ever carried a revolver, loose in your pocket, you know it leaves you self-conscious. It's hard to forget it's there. It makes an insistent weight, heavy against your side, with the coldness of steel. It makes you want to touch it, for some reason. At 8:20 p.m., standing in front of liquor clerk Chuck Morse, Stanley Joiner could not help touching it.

As I pulled my car to the curb in front of the liquor store, I knew by instinct something was wrong in a deadly way. This is a feeling bred of instinct. Reporters who have covered cops, like junkies and prostitutes, can spot an undercover cop at a trouble scene. There were several milling around outside. Inside, one carried a shotgun on his hip.

In the front window of the store, past the cheery orange neon in the front glass, down the neat aisle next to the north wall, 10 feet or more from the front window, Stanley Joiner lay on his back, dying. He was bloody from wounds to his shoulder and back. Medics were beginning to give chest massage. He lay with his shirt off, head back, fast losing touch with this troubled world.

Vice cops with shotguns, tipped off that a robbery was planned at the liquor store, had lain in wait. One officer inside, others outside.

This was the trap that Stanley Joiner walked into. One of his own making, apparently. When he felt that steel-blue revolver in his pocket and pulled it, he jerked the plug, turned the switch, set irrevocably in motion a chain of events that ended, finally, just after 9 p.m. on a stretched white sheet atop a cold steel gurney in the emergency room of Lutheran Hospital.

In the minutes after the shooting, as uniformed cops began to arrive, a tall, burly undercover cop stood in the doorway and refused entrance to the scene. Medics were working feverishly over Joiner. Compress bandages lay red on the floor. A cop walked to the window and blocked the view.

The undercover cop, a short cigar stuck in his mouth, stood with his shoulders back and his hands in the back pockets of his jeans.

"What happened?" he was asked.

"Guy tried to hold up the store," he said. "We got a tip."

"Who shot him? The cops or the clerk?"

The undercover cop looked down in a cold, detached way.

"The cops did," he said. Then he walked away.

The guns were still drawn. The medics pumped the breathing bag to try to bring Joiner back. But two wounds from a shotgun are a hard enemy to fight. And outside, there was a different sentiment. A uniformed cop walked up the concrete apron outside the store to a vice cop.

"Got him, huh?" he said. "Kill him?"

The vice cop murmured something inaudible.

"It'll teach those sons of a bitches a lesson, make 'em think twice," the uniformed cop said. His voice was filled with the anger it takes to kill a man, and the frustration of this hopeless war on crime, where the incredible demand of the job puts a cop behind a shotgun to hide in a liquor store, knowing it might be him on that floor, later, bleeding to death.

But it wasn't. It was Stanley Joiner, a senior at Northside High School when he dropped out two years ago. A nice-looking young man, said the grandmother of one of his friends. He used to come to her house to talk. When he quit school, his friend's grandmother sat in her kitchen and asked him why.

"He said it was his attitude," she said. "I asked him, 'Well, Stanley, can't you change your attitude?' He told me, 'Sure, and I will.' But he wasn't able to. He never did anything real good, to distinguish himself, you know. But he was a polite kid. Real nice spoken, a quiet person. It's too bad."

Joiner was laid off from Superior for two months and hadn't been able to get unemployment compensation yet. His friend's grandmother said he was used to working, having money. He'd been in Boy's School, for trouble before. Maybe crime seemed easy.

Whatever drove him, Stanley Joiner didn't walk into Southwood Park Liquors on a whim. He took a revolver and went to rob. But he told a friend first about his plan. Someone he trusted. The friend told a vice cop. These things happen a lot. Maybe the friend was just trying to save him.

Stanley Joiner didn't own a car. How he got to the liquor store a mile from where he lived, no one seems to know. On the street they say he had a ride. But no one in a car was arrested waiting outside.

It doesn't seem to matter now. All that's known is that he raised his revolver when a cop told him to halt. That was what it took. Then the hammer came down on a short, sad life, and it was over.

FAREWELL TO SPITZ THE CAT

Spitz the cat sat on the railing on the porch of my house, just as the sun was setting Friday night. There was a little breeze blowing and his long brown-and-white fur lay flat. The dry leaves on the ground were stirring and he watched with lazy curiosity. But he did not move.

The yellow street lamps were coming on and the traffic moved nearby on Jefferson Street. I came out of the house on my way back to work and stopped to scratch Spitz's ears. He liked that. I spoke to him and he meowed and I walked down the steps to the truck and left. It was getting dark and there was work to finish.

I did not let Spitz in the house because the evening was nice and he liked to sit out. I wasn't going to be gone long. He always took care of himself. A strong, territorial cat. A hunter. The kind of cat who would walk up to a growling rival, sit down and close his eyes. Fearless. I liked that. I liked Spitz because of it.

A year ago, was an unsettled time at home. Family things. In the middle of that came a special assignment on the old Sheraton Hotel fire. The night that assignment started, Spitz disappeared.

I worried and walked the alleys that night, calling him. For the next three nights I searched. After a week, I feared the worst. After a month, I would only wonder.

One night, writing at home, thinking about him, I started a short story. I called it *Spitz Goes to Paris*. It was about a cat that left home. I guess I was thinking I'd never see Spitz again.

For eight weeks the Sheraton assignment went on, then the first story broke. The first one was the hardest and the writing went on under deadline from early morning until late that night. When I finished about 1 a.m., it was my birthday.

I headed home to an empty house that morning, dead tired, worried about the story and feeling low. As I walked up the steps, there, sitting on the front porch, caterwauling my arrival, was Spitz. Spitz had come home. The world was suddenly brighter.

From then on, it was different with Spitz and me. I never finished the short story about him. But I got it out a few times and he'd sit on the desk like he understood while I'd read it out loud. Corny, maybe, but true.

In the new neighborhood, Spitz didn't go out as much. He hung around, wanting attention. He roamed the apartment, lay in the sun on the side windows, sat on the back porch, watched birds and slept on the foot of the bed. Sometimes he would go out in the yard, down the alley somewhere, but never for long.

Friday night, as I pulled up, a young man from the neighborhood was on my porch. It was about 8:45 p.m. and Paul, who I will always remember for this, came off the steps with the news that something was wrong.

"It's your cat, I think," he said softly. "In the street. It just happened."

I ran down the sidewalk and into Jefferson Street, where the traffic drags its filthy air into this city, where they drive like idiots to beat a stoplight. On the dark pavement under white street lights, I saw Spitz lying.

It was him. The breeze was still blowing and it ruffled his fur. I knelt in the street and could see he was hurt bad and I picked him up easy as I could to lay him on the grass beside the walk.

I put my fingers on his chest but there was nothing. Paul tried, too. There was blood in bad places, but I could not believe. Spitz was too fast, too smart to die like this. Too clever. Too human. But it was true. He was dead.

I brought some white towels down from the house and wrapped them around him because of the blood. I carried him to the house in both arms. I could not believe. He was so soft and warm and peaceful. I pulled the towels around him in a cardboard box and in the truck, we went far out into the country, to the place where he was a kitten. There, at the edge of a woods, in the dark, I dug a place for him.

Mine is a tough business. You see things every day that make you sad and you see hurt and want and it gets you down. Sometimes you see violence and the aftermath of violence and there is blood and death and you learn to live with it because that's the way it is. You're supposed to be hard. Then something like this comes and you wonder how you can feel this way, how it can get you. But it can. When it hits close, it can get you bad.

Last night I sat and thought about Spitz and I missed him. I wanted to see him jump on the desk and sit with his big green eyes wide open. Maybe he was only a cat, but sometimes, if you were feeling like there wasn't a friend in the world, he could jump up and purr and make you scratch his ears, and you'd feel better. I don't know why. But he could.

One of these days, I'm going to finish the short story for Spitz. Maybe it will just go into a drawer. But some years down the road, when I dig it out, I'll remember him for it. Just a personal little thing, for a cat, who was a friend to me. For some reason, I owe him that much. Even if he was just a cat.

AMERICA IS STILL ALIVE AND WELL AT THE MONGO TAVERN

There was a sign on the back of the bar. "In God we Trust – all others pay cash." It meant what it said.

The jukebox came on. It started playing "God Bless America." Loretta put down her cigarette and put her hands in the air. She began to sing. Sarge came up alongside her and in his ragged baritone made an honest harmony.

The occasion was an afternoon in America. The scene was a small town in the heart of some of northern Indiana's most beautiful countryside. The heart of the heart of the country. And in this little tavern, on the corner of two crossroads, America was alive and well.

Sarge, who calls friends by his own nickname, turned to his griddle when the song was done.

"How about that, Sarge," he said, meaning the song. "God bless America, right?"

"Right."

"Somebody better bless her," he said, "'cause she's got troubles now."

Sarge put the steel scraper to the grill, and sent a hamburger sizzling across the hot surface. The sunshine was coming through the window onto the wooden floor in soft yellow squares. The former bomber navigator turned up the fire under his grill.

On the south wall, at the end of the bar, Franklin Delano Roosevelt stared down and across the floor toward the photographs of American B-29s, dropping string after string of bombs on an unseen enemy.

Loretta put another quarter in the old juke and the music filled the room. Someone put money in the bowling machine and the plastic pins made a ratchet-like noise as they descended, the bells of the pin markers chattering.

This was an afternoon like a thousand other afternoons in any part of any year since Sarge and Loretta have guarded, from their own corner of the country, the honor and dignity of America. They, and their Mongo tavern, are one of life's constant things, something that goes unchanged at the heart: the yellow light through the windows, Sarge at the grill and Loretta, keeping track of more than accounts, of the enthusiasm and spirit of the place.

Loretta played one of her favorites, "Ring of Fire." She began to sing again. Her voice had a power to it that was born of conviction. The words filled the high ceilings and surrounded everything within the painted walls. "...and it burned, burned, burned, like a burnin' ring of fire; it went down, down, down, with the flames leapin' higher," Loretta sang, "and it burned, burned, burned the ring of fire... the ring of fire..."

Outside, the lazy, endless state highway wound through the little village, past an abandoned schoolhouse, and the white board chapel with the tall steeple at the edge of town. The steeple was white in the sun and it reached silently toward the dark, bare tree line of a long sloping hill.

The hill lay pretty and brown in the winter sun. Up and down the village streets old houses sat sturdily and rooted in their place. The river, gray-blue in the afternoon light, curved through the millpond and through the town into the spillway that meted out a constant roar and hiss.

Sarge flipped the burger onto a bun and put it on a plate. Loretta carried it to one of the small tables. Sarge's face was a little red from heat. His white shirt stood out against his once-muscular neck. He leaned on the bar and looked tired.

Business remains much the same, but the work grows harder as a man grows older. Even a man like Sarge. He wiped his forehead lightly. He grumbled about the price of hamburger and his cost for beer. He grumbled about the small businessman and the help he doesn't get.

"This is a great country, Sarge," he said. "But we've got a lot of trouble. Too many people out of work. How's a man going to make it, and this Social Security thing, why..." He threw down with both hands and turned his back.

"Somethin's got to give, Sarge," he said. "Somethin's got to give."

Loretta handed him an order and he went back to his work. She slipped another coin in the jukebox. America the Beautiful. She put her cigarette down and began to sing.

PITY THE THIEVES THE JUNKMAN OUTSMARTED

The Junk Man was spending his Sunday working in his yard. He was not planting flowers. He was wrestling two rusty old engine blocks into the back of a pickup truck for hauling, and dragging oily bits and parts of machinery out of a tumbledown garage. He was doing this to relax.

Fritz, the junkyard dog, kept a constant pace on a short chain. He was a handsome dog for his ilk, well-spoken and the kind to leave a clear impression upon a visitor.

"Fritz, now quiet," the Junk Man said. "He barks more when I'm here than when I'm gone."

"He wants to show he earns his keep," it was suggested.

"He earns his keep," the Junk Man said.

One time, some years ago, Fritz was guarding the often-vacant property where the Junk Man stores his valuables. But his chain was so short that some clever thieves took advantage and began regularly siphoning gas from the Junk Man's trucks.

"I came to get a truck one day, always kept them filled up then, and drove down the street half a mile and ran out of gas. It happened a couple more times, and then a battery disappeared."

The Junk Man thought about this for a while and then he went to a store and did two things. He bought a big can of fuel oil and a brand new battery with bright shiny cables.

He put the battery in the dead truck and wheeled it around facing the street. Then he put the hood up on the truck so the battery was clearly visible from the street. He also added about 40 feet to Fritz's chain.

"The next morning I came out and found the battery cables cut and one bolt loosened," he said. "But I also found the back pocket of a pair of blue jeans lying on the ground nearby and quite a bit of blood on the ground. I think Fritz must have taken them by surprise. Never lost another battery."

For the gas thieves, however, he had a better plan. One evening he filled each of the trucks with fuel oil and shorted Fritz's chain. Early the next morning the Junk Man went shopping for his crook.

"I found an old car sitting by the road nearby with nobody around, so I took off the gas cap and smelled it. It was fuel oil all right," the Junk Man said.

Ironically, he'd seen the car before and knew where the owner worked. So, he dropped by to see him.

"I told him I saw his car out on the road and he said his boy had been driving it when it quit."

"I asked him what went wrong, and he said his boy didn't know, it just up and quit running. He was going down later to take a look."

"I told him when he got to checking he'd probably find his boy had stolen some bad gas. But this made him indignant. He said if I was calling his boy a thief, I'd damn well better be able to prove it."

"So, I made him a deal. I said if he'd come down and look at the car, and if we drained the tank and put gas in it, and it started, I'd let him pay to fill my trucks back up, pay for the fuel oil. I said if he'd do that, I'd forget it and let him deal with his boy himself."

The plan worked.

"I don't know what he ever did to the boy," the Junk Man said. "But I bet he got the daylights whaled out of him.

"And I do know this much," the Junk Man said. "I never lost any more gas either."

ONCE LIFE HUMMED LIKE FAT TIRES DOWN A DARK HIGHWAY

Go a long way back. Go back into the memory. Deeply, down the long corridors of the mind, into the dim chambers and caverns. Go back to childhood and pull something out. Pick a day, or a time, an hour, a moment. Pull all the colors out, the temperature, the sound, the emotion of the moment, the way the sky looked. What do you have?

I remember something out of the long past. It starts on a state highway north of Huntington. Some of the memory, perhaps, is like jargon is to language, a created thing. But it circles round a central core, a picture in the mind, and grows from there.

I remember standing on the floor of the car, a Chevrolet I think, standing on the floor by the transmission hump, back of the knees against the back seat, chest against the front seat, barely able to see over, father and mother in the front seat, the car rolling with the hum of fat tires on asphalt. A dark night.

There was a curve in the road, a long sweeping curve and deep ditches, ravine-like, on either side. We rolled to a stop in the middle of the dark countryside behind a line of cars, 20 or 30, headlights on. Something was ahead.

My father got out. You could see the cars a long way ahead. He walked on the berm side, though no cars came from the other direction. He was gone and then he came back. "It's an accident," he said.

A car had gone off into the ditch, through the trees, crashing a guard rail, tumbling before sliding into a streambed, lights pointing into the dark sky. We could not see the car. The police had not come and passersby had gotten out to help. My father left the car again. Someone had heard a child crying in the ravine. They made a search party.

It seemed like a long time. Maybe it was minutes. He came back and got into the car. They found nothing, but the police had come. We sat longer and then began to move, slowly. From the roadside window, where I looked out, there was a body in the middle of the highway. Someone had covered it with a green wool Army blanket. The man, you could see, lay face down, his arms above his head. I do not know how I knew it was a man. Perhaps the size. There was no blood. His fingers stuck out above the blanket.

We moved on into the night. The line of cars broke up, the night air washing over us. I stood looking out the window for a long time, not seeing the night but seeing the green blanket in the road. They never found a child. Someone else was hurt or killed. I don't remember. There was no ambulance.

Knitted into this memory are strange and unconnected events. Bits and pieces of the past that are said to shape us, give rise to our fears and our confidence. Accidents have always made me anxious. In later years, as a reporter, I covered hundreds of them, blood and death and common but terrible ironies so companion to such disaster.

But none of those tragedies stick in the mind like the one on that seasonless night, in the memory, where some nameless person died and life went on, humming like fat tires, taking the long dark highway home.

Funny what the memory keeps. Funny, too, what it throws away.

FIRST GRADERS LIKE NEWSPAPERS
– MAINLY COMICS

When they came in from recess, their cheeks were the color of apples, and their eyes watered. They hung their coats on the hooks on the wall and moved toward their little desks. Their names were printed on cards taped at the corners of their desks.

Some of them sat down right away. Others walked curiously up to look over their guest, who sat in a wooden chair at the front of the room. Their teacher, Eleanor Robinson, greeted them at the door and helped them with their coats.

"Today we have a guest whom we talked about earlier this morning," she began. They were all in their seats now, some squirming, some silently still.

The guest, a reporter, sat quietly.

"We're going to talk about cats this morning. Maybe you would like to tell (the reporter) some cat stories of your own," Robinson said.

Hands shot up around the room.

"I had a kitten and it got run over by a car," said one little girl. She was wearing a red dress and her mother had apparently pinned a white sweater together for her at the neck. She had a tiny voice.

"My cat jumps up on the refrigerator and we put her food bowl up there so the dog won't eat it," said another girl.

In the back of the room a projector was ready to roll. The reel was from the Lost Angeles Humane Shelter and was about a cat named Priscilla. The film was shot from the vantage point of the cat; you could see the way the world looked to a cat. Cute. In the end, the cat was nabbed by the humane shelter and locked up.

The reporter moved his chair out of the way and watched. A tow-headed boy next to him stared quietly with wide eyes, not at the movie but at the reporter.

When the film was over and the talk of cats was finished, the teacher asked if the class would like to ask some questions about newspapers. The reporter sat forward in his chair. He called on one boy named John.

"Why do they make the words so little," the boy named John wanted to know. The reporter scratched his head.

"Why don't they print the newspaper in color?" asked another boy. The reporter scratched his head again.

"How do you print a newspaper?" asked a little girl. The reporter tried to explain what a cylinder was, but he gave up. There were lots of questions. The reporter was scratching himself bald. He decided to take a readership survey.

"How many of you look at the newspaper at home," he asked. More than half of the hands went up, but a reporter is always skeptical.

"What do you look at in the newspaper?" he asked.

"The comics," a little girl said. "The comics," echoed another.

"Do you look at pictures?" the reporter asked, being clever.

"Yes!" they said. "The comic pictures!"

"Garfield!" yelled a little girl in the front row. "I like Garfield!"

They were back to cats.

The reporter stood up to go, but the teacher handed him some flash cards. They were subtraction flash cards. It took the reporter longer to subtract than the kids. This was first grade.

"They practice all the time," the reporter told himself.

Finally, it was over. The reporter went outside into the cold air where his checks turned the color of apples. He was thinking about all the potential newspaper readers inside. He shook his head.

"Comics," he said. "Very funny."

AN ICONOCLASTIC NEWSMAN
CALLS IT QUITS

Something will go out of the newspaper business tomorrow afternoon. Nobody will see it go. It will go out on the coattails of Mr. Norman Carter, iconoclast, who, after 45 years in this business, will hang up his copy pencil and retire.

I could tell you a lot of things about Norman Carter: that he is a very funny man, that he is greatly loved among staffers in the News Sentinel newsroom, that he has a sly innocence and a boyishness that charms people, and that he can drink any given quantity of beer and still spell every word in the dictionary.

But those things won't tell you anything about what I'd like to say, which is something about the business of newspapering and how it relates to Norman Carter's view of the world.

For 45 years Norman has had a ringside seat on the human condition. Sure, he's labored long nights, struggling with some fact crying to be uncovered. And he's witnessed countless hours editing loosely written, uninspired copy, the grist for the mill of daily journalism. But he did it for love, not money.

That's why something goes out of journalism tomorrow. Norman Carter is among the last of a disappearing breed, the self-taught, ambulance-chasing, learn-it-on-the-street reporter-editor. That was the standard back in 1937 when Norman walked in the door of a newsroom and went to work.

Norman Carter allowed Indiana University to present its case for one year and then expelled it from his life. He did graduate high school, though at times he claimed to be an elementary school dropout. No one taught him the essence of a lead paragraph in school, nor the mysteries of syntax, nor why some words sound better strung together than others.

All that came through intuition, experience, emotion and a feeling for this work. It came when there was more of a mystery to this business itself, when reporters tended, as a lot, to be hard drinkers, courageous at seeing life at its ugliest, most raw, and unspeakable.

The stereotype did exist. Reporters who were tough talking, aggressive, eccentric. Skeptical. Suspicious. Members of a fraternity that watched out for its own.

Things have changed somewhat. You can't get work on a daily newspaper anymore with guts, self-education and a flair for writing. The first thing they look for is a college degree.

Gone also are the days of copy paper cut from end rolls of newsprint and typewritten copy edited with a pencil beneath a shaded bulb. Linotypes are gone. Computers handle copy. Hot type is a thing of the past. Much of the aura of the business he loved is gone. Soon Norman will be gone, too.

There are a few things wrong with expecting college graduates to hit the streets with versatility that comes with age. But age is not respected any longer.

Already in college there is specialization. Reporters/editors come onto a newspaper and are prepared to cover education or government, with an idea that textbook journalism approximates the real world.

Not that there aren't good reporters among them. But as their need for intuition and resourcefulness is diminished, their testing comes from classrooms, not deadlines. They tend to place more credence in government than people. It is a world too polite, too elevated to deal with the dirty work of politics and the human condition.

Some journalists now come to their jobs with law degrees. This is touted as good, an answer to media irresponsibility. I doubt it.

There is only one thing that matters, and that's getting the facts straight. And that's what Norman Carter learned on the street and behind the desk and the thing he tried to make important.

That effort to get the facts straight won't go out the door when Norman Carter leaves the office for the last time tomorrow. But some of the spirit, the rough and tumble journalism, the scuffling kind of spirit that attracted mavericks and skeptics to this business will go out with him.

I will miss his off-color jokes, his shuffling innocence, his wit and felicity with language. Norman used to write a column for this newspaper, and it was one of the best things ever to appear here.

When he quit wiring, his column was replaced with Street Talk. He helped shape and guide that replacement with the generosity and spirit that made the newspaper business what it used to be: the passing of the chalice, the honor of craftsmanship, from one generation to another.

But things change, times change, perspectives change. You can't stand in the way. You can only step aside, and watch it go.

This is the way it will be tomorrow afternoon when Norman Carter goes out the door. He will go, and take a piece of the business with him.

PUTTING A REIN ON THE FEARS OF LITTLE BOYS

Fear is a strange thing. Part emotion, part chemistry. An essential ingredient in most people's lives. A healthy thing when it warns you of danger. And unhealthy if it takes control of a person's life, which is a thing that can happen.

I was lying in bed the other night with a storm coming up and I began to think about fear. Thunder was on the roll and the wind was rising. It came slow and turned steady, then ominous in the dark.

It did not bother me to lie in bed and listen to the wind. I've come to like the wind. But it reminded me of something. Of a father and a son and little story about fear.

The boy was just a kid then, 8 or 9, I guess. But since he was old enough to talk, he'd been frightened of storms. The other things in his young life seemed under control. School was all right. He was active. Good at most everything he tried, in fact. And confident.

But when a wind was rising and the clouds moved in, the boy would grow quiet. He'd find a place to sit where he did not have to see the storm, or hear the wind. When it thundered, he would begin to cry. And if the storm was bad, he'd find his father and cling to him while the fear ravaged him.

His father always told him, "There's nothing to be afraid of son, settle down and find something to do.' The boy would go off then and try to do as his father said. But all he could do was sit in his room and tremble, trying to choke off the sobs until the storm blew over.

It puzzled the father, this fear. He had been afraid of storms once himself. In fact, he still got a little uneasy about them sometimes if the wind was particularly violent. But he'd been so careful not to let the boy see fear in him that he couldn't understand it. Still, he often blamed himself when his son was terrified.

Instead of going away, though, the fear got worse. Now, when the storms came up, the boy didn't cling to his father. But he'd sit nearby, his face in his hands, quivering on the edge of panic.

One evening a storm came suddenly and the sky went a sickly yellow color. The humid air would not stir and when the rain came it drove in torrents. The power went down, came on again, and went out completely. In the yard of the house across the street, a small tree came up by its roots and fell in the drive.

"Come and look at the storm," the father said. But the boy could not. His father took him by the arm and tried to bring him gently to the window, but the boy cried so hard he got sick. He began to throw up, choking and coughing. It shocked his father, frightened him in the way a father can be frightened for his child. He decided then he had to do something.

He thought about it for a long time. The next time it stormed, he was ready.

"Listen son," he told the uneasy boy as the storm moved in. "Doesn't it make you angry that the wind does this to you? Don't you ever get angry at the storm for frightening you so much?"

The boy had never thought of this. He shrugged his shoulders. Already his lower lip was out and quivering.

"You and I are going to go out and have a talk with the wind," his father said. "Come on, we're going to take care of this once and for all."

He took the boy in his arms and carried him outside far from the house toward the woods. There was a hill. The lightning was a long way off and the thunder rolled. The wind gusted and spit rain. The father put the boy down and turned with his face to the wind and shook his fist.

"I'm angry with you for frightening my son," he yelled into the growing storm. "And we're not going to put up with it anymore, do you hear me? Blow as hard as you want. We're not afraid of you!"

He yelled loud and deep and with a great passion and then he turned to the boy. "Stand up to the wind son," he said. "Stand up to it."

A look came over the boy's face. A strange and brave little look and he half laughed and half cried and began shouting at the wind at the top of his lungs. Suddenly they were both laughing and yelling, urging the storm on, and the father bent and scooped the boy up, hugged him hard and they ran back, laughing under the rain.

The fear didn't go completely away, of course. But the boy was changed after that. When the storms came, he'd go to the window and his father would hear him, telling the night that he wasn't afraid. Later he came to love the sound of the wind. And he really wasn't afraid anymore.

I like to think about that story, sometimes, lying in bed in the night when storms come. It makes me feel good to remember it. And it also reminds me that any fear can fall in the face of a little courage.

Part 4

In the Shadows of Fame and Famousness

Street Talk's author would write about occasional encounters with the famous, and often in descriptions of the day-to-day world around them. A table next to Ted Kennedy in Chicago during the presidential campaign, covering the visit of Mother Teresa, reporting on the shooting in Fort Wayne of civil rights leader Vernon Jordan. Eight years after the column on Kennedy, he would find himself investigating the famous Senator in a far different context. - HMC

FOR KENNEDY, THE CAMPAIGN NEVER REALLY STOPS

CHICAGO – It was early in the evening and already there was a small crowd inside Dianna's Opaa in Greektown. Petros Kogiones was moving around nervously. The waiters in their white aprons and shirts were watching him. They knew who was coming and they knew this Saturday would be a little different and it made them uneasy, too.

Petros was standing in the entryway and right away you could see he was ready for something. He kept brushing his long, black hair off the collar of his black suit jacket. There was a silk handkerchief in his jacket pocket and he was wearing a tie. He looked tense and he was moving quickly.

He said something in Greek to one of his waiters The waiter moved like had been shot across the broad dining room floor, through the wide double doors into the kitchen. Petros started looking for flowers. Then he saw someone he had seen in the restaurant before, Donna Craven, with Jim Looman. He put his arm around Donna and walked with her into the dining room.

"Do you like Ted Kennedy?" he said to her quietly.

"I like your restaurant," she said.

"No, I'm serious. Do you like Ted Kennedy? Does everyone in your party like him? Good. I will seat you as close as I can tonight. But there must be no heckling, all right?"

He walked with her across the room to a far corner which was near the kitchen doors but was also beside the raised area with the iron railing around it. He held her chair.

"You will like it here," he said. "But there must be no heckling. I trust you."

He smiled his handsome, Greek smile and then moved off quickly, shouting in Greek to another waiter and pointing to the table. The waiters had congregated in a small group and were talking, watching the door.

People began to file in. The flowers arrived. Petros unwrapped them and shoved them down into a vase, bunched together. Two dozen carnations in one, a dozen roses in the other. A young woman from Fort Wayne who was at the Craven-Looman table, got up and came to arrange the flowers. Petros was glad to have the detail off his hands because the Secret Service agents were beginning to come in and they wanted to talk to him.

There was a round table at the far end of the platform. There were a half-dozen long square tables, too. The round table was against one wall. The Secret Service agents walked through the restaurant and one of them walked along the back wall where Kennedy would be sitting and pounded on it with his hands to see if it was solid. Satisfied, he moved to a far corner, pulled a small microphone from inside his suit pocket, and spoke into it.

Around the restaurant, patrons who did not know Kennedy was coming were ordering their dinners. Flaming appetizers were being served with cries of "Opaa!" The Secret Service men watched everything.

Petros went through his last-minute preparations. He told the waiters he would serve the Kennedy party himself. He was still attending to the small things when the Secret Service began to move toward the door. The harsh television lights on the sidewalk outside spilled through the thrust-open door and heads began to turn. Kennedy came in surround by agents, his children and members of the Shriver family right behind him. Petros greeted them at the door, then, as they stepped into the hall, people began to get to their feet and applaud. The entire restaurant was on its feet. The noise was deafening.

Kennedy swept through the crowd and he grabbed hands stuck awkwardly in front of him. The national media was hard on his heels and there were still bright television camera lights following him as he made his way toward the table where he sat with his back to a wall- a human wall of agents between him and the other patrons. Kennedy's face looked deeply tired under the searing-white camera lights. He touched a hundred hands in a few seconds. Then he was away from the crowd. The agents moved to the table in front of him and sat on the edge of their seats. They scanned the crowd. They would keep it up for the next two hours.

Petros was yelling instructions and things were happening fast. Red wine was coming to the table. Red caviar and flaming cheese in brandy. Petros talked with Kennedy and they embraced and there were smiles and inaudible talk, and then Petros went to the center of his restaurant. He went to make his announcement to his captive audience. He had stuck a thick cigar into his mouth, unlit, and now he held it in one hand and began to talk. It was his turn to be politician.

"Dianna's Opaa tries to bring you, our friends, the best..." he began. He looked down at brief notes. "...without you there would be no Dianna's, and without you there would be nothing...even the Senator from Massachusetts has come here. What more do you want...?"

He was drawing laughs from the crowd and then he introduced Kennedy without endorsement, and a man who had been drinking much wine shouted something against him. The man was booed. Petros ignored it. The senator stood and came to the railing. The agents slipped off their chairs and came forward, nervously.

All day in Chicago, as he prepared for the Illinois primary, Kennedy had been with Jessie Jackson and minority rights leaders, with blacks and with the poor, saying none of them had received due consideration from the Carter administration. Now, in the most popular of Greek restaurants in Greektown, he said he had only come to enjoy.

"We did not come to campaign tonight," he said, cameras flashing, Klieg lights blazing. "We came, like you, because we heard that Dianna's Opaa has the best Greek food...We want tonight to be like any other night at Dianna's..."

But it was not. Not quite.

An older, white-haired man in a gray suit, a knit white shirt beneath his jacket, had gone with Petros up the steps onto the raised dining area and the Secret Service agents had stopped them. There had been a discussion. Now Bob Papademas, who was as famous to the people in Greektown as Kennedy, sat by himself with a long cigar in his hand and at a table where there was a telephone and he waited.

Papademas had been on the radio in Greece when the world war had come. He was a freedom fighter and a proud man and he had been a man of the radio for more than 40 years. He had seen many things. Now he waited patiently until the man who wanted to be president had a few minutes. He did not light his cigar. He drank water.

Finally, the senator left his table, the agents circling around him, and he sat down beside Papademas. He unbuttoned his coat and they talked. An aide listened and took notes. There was to be no campaigning, but there was always campaigning like this, the most important kind, the kind with people like Papademas, who could help.

Later, as he sat alone again near the kitchen doors, Papademas looked around the room and he said what he believed.

"The Greeks, they will vote for him," he said. "We backed Carter, but he forgot his promises to us. He was afraid of Iran. Now we have someone who is not afraid. Now we believe in Kennedy."

The senator stood to leave, finally, after a toast with Ouzo, a Greek liquor sent in the bottle to his table by the throng of media people who had been seated completely across the room. Kennedy came down the steps and the Secret Service formed tightly around him. They went out through the crowd together.

Petros stood nearby, near the kitchen, and the tension that had been on his face went out of it. There had been nothing dangerous. No incidents. Now it was over.

He smiled and looked across the room.

"We rise above politics here," he said. "I told him, if Jimmy Carter wants to come, we welcome him too, the same way. We leave the door open for the President."

He walked across the floor and kissed a woman who had just come in the door.

REAGAN AND THE RAGGED PEOPLE

INDIANAPOLIS – I'm just writing this memo to the city desk and then I'm going to forget it and go down to Irene's Lounge where Chip Edwards used to hang out, and watch this aftermath of a presidential visit.

It was too cold to go out on the streets in Indianapolis today but that is where the real action was, not in the Statehouse, where Ronald Reagan stood and talked for a half hour or so about giving power back to "the people" in Indiana.

I did not hear this in person, but rather on a television set in a place called the Clique Cocktail Lounge, which is just off Market at Illinois Street and is a place where women dance in back and take off their shirts.

I went in to see the ragged street people who were trying to get out of the cold wind for a few minutes at a time. They came in and cruised the long, tacky aisle, turned and stood, looking like they lost something, or were looking for somebody. Then they'd shoot a glance at Darlene or Carla on the stage and turn around and walk very slowly out the door.

They were doing this little stroll because they could not afford the price of a drink. Those who could were at the bar in front of the television, waiting on the President's plane and, later, on the speech, which would not get a good reception in the Clique.

One of the guys at the bar had worked in a foundry in Tennessee. He was in the Clique now because he did not have work, and he told this to a black man sitting beside him. The black man said he was waiting on a bus himself, heading toward Fort Wayne, because he thought he'd find work there.

"Maybe Ronald Reagan gives you a job," the black man said.

"Reagan don't have nothing for me," said the guy from Tennessee. Then he got down off his stool and walked to the back where he could watch the girls at their sullen work.

The girls were tired and bored and were playing slow, easy, rolling country music, dancing a slow, rolling style that meant this was the end of the line and it did not look good from here.

All this was a block from the Capitol building where 200 out of work machinists and auto workers and electrical workers from Kokomo and Anderson and elsewhere stood outside venting anger and frustration.

There was some shouting and a woman named Jill Chambers got up and said a few words about the NOW organization and then about work and home and families and about how Reagan didn't seem to care about the women and elderly, and children, and that's why he didn't mind dumping social programs onto the states which lost them in the first place because they didn't do the job right.

She was shouting against the cold wind, and she choked a little and coughed and said she was sorry.

"I've got pneumonia," she yelled. "Does anybody want it?"

"Give it to Reagan," someone in the crowd yelled back.

From the limestone steps that looked out toward Monument Circle you could see the late lunch crowd coming under the rich blue awning of the private, exclusive Columbia Club.

The shouting and the chants echoed to Meridian Street, with talk about Reagan's attitude toward the poor and distressed, the out-of-work, the growing tide of humanity unsatisfied and unsettled and looking for hope.

But it wasn't those people that Reagan saw or heard. He came in on the other side of the Capitol Building, moving fast with Secret Service agents riding the limousine running boards, their black coats flapping against white shirts in the bitter wind.

The people Reagan saw walked smartly across the hallowed marble Statehouse halls in suits and dresses, and they had tickets and passes to see the President. The State Police ringed the Capitol and kept out the less privileged.

When Reagan appeared on the television screen the applause from the House floor went on for 45 seconds or more. In his long-practiced smile you could see reflected the mandate of the people of Indiana who sat before him.

But in the streets of Indianapolis, the dwindling crowd of disillusioned poor and unemployed, who knew they would not be seen or heard, stood silently in the cold. The dancers at the Clique went on, bored and at the bottom of life's little insults, and a man whose face was reddened by the wind carried a cardboard sign saying "We want jobs not cheese."

Inside the warm House chamber, Reagan said he had come to find out what the people of Indiana wanted. But nobody came outside to ask if anybody had questions for the President.

Reagan said he knew Hoosiers wanted a chance to control their own destiny without the federal government interfering.

What it looked like they wanted outside in the cold was something more immediate than rhetoric.

When it was all over the President came out to his motorcade and it skirted small crowds at corners, moving fast around to Washington and West streets. No one was there waiting to see the president. Just two reporters and two cops directing traffic. Reagan leaned forward in the limousine and waved. No one waved back.

This is what I saw and heard and what I had a feeling it was going to be like. I never picked up my press pass, incidentally. Like I said, everything you needed to know about New Federalism and Reaganomics was out on the street, in the cold, in places where hope got nothing for its trouble Tuesday. You really didn't need a press pass from the President to go find that.

A FAITH THAT MOVES MOUNTAINS
MOVES AN AUDIENCE TO TEARS

The Rev. Richard McGuire, a prior of the Crosier Center, stood on the platform in front of the stage in the auditorium at Bishop Dwenger High School.

It was 2 p.m. on a beautiful Sunday and his job was brief, but eloquent. It left him smiling with a gracefulness that spoke to the moment at hand. A moment much awaited among the Crosier fathers and brothers, and the community. A small and breathless moment.

In the wings, between the curtains of the stage, Mother Teresa of Calcutta, the living saint, peacemaker, honored by the world in the name of the poor with the Nobel Prize for peace, stood waiting; the woman whose simple faith in Christ proved so strong, so pure, that it changed the lives of millions of people and captured the attention of the world.

In the minutes to come, Mother Teresa, with the same quiet power that has moved mountains, would move 3,000 people in the Dwenger auditorium to tears of joyfulness, would lift their spirits and make them feel loved.

But on the brink of this one moment, as Father McGuire spoke, a miracle of faith had already unfolded for the Crosiers, for the Catholic community, and for the City of Churches itself. The great peace-maker, living saint, was in their midst. And the feeling was a strong current that washed away the world outside.

"God surprised us," the Rev. James Vedro said in preface to McGuire's remarks. "He surprised us by sending us this simple, pure woman ... to teach us not to be afraid of the poor ... for they have something to give to us."

They called the visit a special blessing on the community, and as the dignitaries of the church sat in black suits and white collars, in the wings of the stage, her head down in the attitude of constant prayer, Mother Teresa, lion of courage, dove of humility, stood, lips moving, hands clasping her small rosary.

In a few seconds, the crowd would rise to its feet. But at this moment she was alone with God, sturdy sandals on her feet, the hood of her white and blue sari covering her forehead to just above the eyes, and a simple gray sweater clinging to her rounded shoulders. A look of peace was on her face.

Father McGuire finished his simple introduction, then the living saint, a symbol of hope in a troubled world, walked from the wings onto the stage, down the steps to the platform, into the bright lights of television cameras, and into the hearts of people.

Despite her 71 years, so many of them lived in Calcutta's squalid streets, Mother Teresa moved strongly to the platform, an athlete of the spirit, eyes down, heart strong and poised on the brink of a beautiful and familiar litany, about to share the love for which she lives.

First she prayed. Her voice was a lilting thing. The words from her mouth were simple as her robe, but the people on bleachers strained forward to hear and sat, as though stunned, perfectly still. The words, as soft as whispers, came clear as a cold, rushing stream. Every eye was on this woman of God.

Outside in the parking lot, uniformed police officers stood guard. Through an open door at the side of the auditorium, the breeze of a perfect day flowed and carried the gentle crackling of a distant police radio.

Plainclothes officers, street-wise men, stood in the halls and in the auditorium, unseen and armed to protect her. But they were not needed. As she spoke of faith that every child of God is precious to Him, it was clear she needed only that faith to protect her.

What struck you, then, was the enormity of what this great faith had done. It had brought peace to the dying, health to the sick, food to the hungry. Now it was bringing hope to people weary of a different kind of sickness, from loneliness, fear of tomorrow, and lives lived with emptiness.

There was no emptiness in the words of Mother Teresa. She told stories of the street. Her life, full, rich, overflowing, spilled into the auditorium and the words were welcomed as though something was healed by words alone, and by this sense of faith, of peace and the work to be done. A great feeling of goodwill settled on the assembly, a feeling of optimism and of courage.

For 30 minutes, she spoke. It went so quickly. Then Mother Teresa closed with a prayer and climbed the steps to the stage. The people stood and did the only thing they knew to do. They applauded. On and on. Then some began to move forward, quickly, anxiously, and a woman with a child went up onto the platform and up the stage and Mother Teresa spoke to the child and touched her.

Then people pushed forward, onto the platform and stage, looking for a word, a touch from the living saint. She took their hands, smiling in a way that, once seen, could not be forgotten.

Soon Mother Teresa will be back in the streets of Calcutta. In her brief visit here, she brought that world to our doorstep, and made us perhaps, more sensitive to the needs of the poor, the need for brotherhood and the rewards of sharing. With a single thread of faith, a needle of truth, she stitched these two worlds a little closer together. It is clear she touched the heart of this community. And left it, some now say, with a great legacy of love.

A HOT DAY ON PONTIAC STREET,
NO ANSWERS

It is early afternoon, no breeze blowing.

"A hot one today," says the man in the truck. He looks across the seats. I look out the window. We are looking for a man down on Pontiac Street.

The sun comes down bright, hits the sidewalk, white. Heat shimmers off car hoods, sinks into asphalt.

"We'll look here a minute," he says. "You wait here."

Truck at the curb, he goes into a cool, dark place and looks. Man's not there.

"Lot of people on the street today," says the man getting into the truck.

I shrug. We are looking for just one man. To ask him a question. A question only he can answer.

"We go down by his place?" the man in the truck asks, cigarette in his mouth, sweat on his lip. We cruise the long street. It's hot, the sweat is running. Truck's hot. No breeze blowing.

"Here's his boys," says the man in the truck. He pulls very slowly to the curb, gets out.

"Hey buddy," I hear him yell. He walks to the side of a car, kind of swaggers. The car is sagging at the curb. Looks like its axle's broken.

I can't hear the conversation. He puts his hands on the car door by the window but the metal is too hot. Inside the car, two men look at him, slow and cool.

The sidewalk is all traffic. Men on the street corners standing around. People on the porches of stores and barbershops. Sun's hot. Bright. Something's hanging humid in the air.

The man in the truck gets back in the truck. Kind of quiet.

"Bein' funny today," he says. "Not very friendly to questions. Maybe it's too hot to talk, heh? Gets too hot down here sometimes."

We go down the street. The man we are looking for is not at his place. The dirt in the gutter on Pontiac Street comes up in a brown little twister. Grit nicks the truck, wind picks loose paper and whirls it round.

"One place left."

We go slowly down the street. He sticks his head out the window.

"Hey, junkie!!!" he yells. He's laughing. They both laugh.

"Where's my man?"

The man in the street shrugs to the man in the truck and turns his palms up in the sun. His heavy stocking cap in the heat is soaked in sweat like a foundryman's. Sidewalk's bright. We all squint on down the street.

Something cool comes on a breeze. People walk slow, easy, no-place-no-hurry, everything's cool. Woman in bright red shorts and heels struts the street. Man in a straw hat, easy in the shade. Somebody sits on the curb, head down. Something on the breeze cools sweat on the brow and clouds come up.

We come to the last place. The man in the truck goes in. There is a cool, cool breeze down Pontiac now and the sky goes brooding dark. Air hangs, heavy, sweet. Storm coming. People rock on porches. Walk on sidewalks. Everybody outside looking in the heat. Big rain coming.

The man in the truck comes back. Gets in.

"Can't find your man," he says. "Maybe he be outta' town."

He puts the truck in gear and leans his head out the window. Storm's coming up. People crowd into sagging doorways. Everything's cool.

"Gonna get no answer to your question today," the man in the truck says.

I nod. You can hear the thunder. Rain splats the windshield in big gray drops, and then it's pouring.

Part 5

The Frankie Columns

"Frankie" was a character in a set of columns that captured the author's own fanciful sense of exaggerated humor. Those columns were primarily inspired by another well-known Hoosier newsman of the era, the late Mike Dooley, whose own sense of humor and Irish antics were legendary in newsrooms around the state. 'Frankie' has never been identified, until now, and on some rare occasions other persons might have assumed a Frankie-like role through the keystrokes of the author, all for the sake of capturing a satirical tale in good fun. But Frankie 'was' Dooley and Dooley was always, the author said, a reliable source of humor.
— HMC

RADISH RACE CURES BLUES FOR FRANKIE

My good friend Frankie and I were sitting in the kitchen Sunday afternoon with the window open. We'd planned to have a picnic in the yard and play croquet, but the sun wouldn't come out. No amount of coaxing could get Frankie to picnic under a cloudy sky.

"Next you'll want to do it without ants," he sniffed.

Frankie has been in a bad mood lately. He gets like this now and then. Only some insanity can cheer him up. I had been working for weeks at getting him out of this funk, when at last a solution was reached.

"Listen," I said. "Let's put in a joint garden this year. I've got the soil ready; all we have to do is plant."

"Plant the garden?" he said, with raised eyebrow. "It might rain."

"Best time to plant," I told him, though I was guessing.

"What phase is the moon?" he asked.

"Dark. It's the dark of the moon," I said. "Best time to plant."

"But I'd get my hands dirty," he said. "All week I'd have to clean my fingernails."

"No, you won't," I said. "I'll give you soap. Let's go get some seeds and plant."

He mulled it over.

"Oh, all right," he said finally. "I'll go along. But I'm not planting. You plant. I can't get excited about it."

We got in the car and went to the closest seed store. The place was packed with would-be planters.

"Look at all these people," Frankie said. "Lot of gardeners this year."

He wandered up the aisle and I looked at the seeds. Suddenly Frankie walked up with a package.

"Look at this," he said. "I think I found something to plant."

"I looked at the package. It was a different color from the rest of the packages in the rack. I pointed this out.

"It was the last one," he said. "But look what it says on the back."

I looked on the back at the tiny print. In very small letters it said, "Giant Radishes."

"Giant radishes?" I asked.

"Yeah," Frankie said. His eyes were lighting up. "Giant Radishes."

He grabbed the package and read it out loud.

"Four-Pound Radishes, and Larger," he read. "Giant Radishes."

For some reason, giant radishes had grabbed his imagination and shaken loose his lethargy. He was getting enthusiastic.

"Come on," he said. "Let's get started. It might be a short growing season."

He hurried up to the checkout and paid for the seeds. I followed him out the door to the car. He threw the bag in the parking lot and started reading the package again.

"Listen," he said, "we've got to give these radishes extra-special treatment. We could grow the biggest radish in town. Maybe in the whole county! We'll get our pictures in the newspaper."

"Great," I said. "Why don't we do better than that? Why don't we challenge anybody in town to grow a bigger radish? The Great Radish Contest."

"Eureka!" Frankie yelled. "It's a project."

The minute we got back Frankie jumped out of the car and rushed into the back yard. By the time I got there he was gently patting the earth on top of the seeds.

"Okay," he said breathlessly, brushing the dirt from his hands. He stood over the spot with the hoe in his hand.

"Let's challenge everybody we know to grow a bigger radish than us."

"Right," I said. "Then we'll water it every day. Give it some special fertilizer."

"Only the best," Frankie said. "We'll put our giant radish against the biggest homegrown radish in town. Winner takes 'em both."

That did it and now I'm afraid it's truly a contest. Frankie says he's spreading the word at work, trying to get contestants, and I said I'd tell everybody I could.

So, if you can grow a bigger radish than Frankie and me, give us a call in August. Until then, we'll be hanging around, growing the biggest radish you ever saw.

THE GARDENER'S SANDBAGS

Day before yesterday I was sitting on my front porch, watching the rain clouds in gathering fury drift over the city, when my good friend Frankie drove up.

"Come on," he yelled from the street. "Get out here and give me a hand."

There were raindrops spitting through the trees and everything was muggy. Frankie threw open his truck and pulled out a sandbag.

"Help me get these out back," he said as I walked down the porch steps. "Hurry up."

He went off toward the backyard at a serious clip, with me close behind.

"Where did you get that?" I asked, pointing at the sandbag. "You didn't steal any from Franke Park, did you?"

"Naw," Frankie said. "I got these a long time ago from the dikes. And it's a good thing cause now we need 'em. It's gonna flood."

The sky did look dark and threatening. There were severe storm warnings out. And it had been raining for days. Ever since the Great Flood, my neighbors and I suffered from that malady, (perhaps a phobia), known as "Fear of Flooding." But Frankie was carrying things to extreme.

"You've only got a dozen sandbags," I said. "What good will that do?"

"Plenty," said Frankie, "if you'd quit talking and get to work."

He eyed the threatening sky and hurried, as fast as he could, which isn't very, back for more bags. To humor him I grabbed a couple.

"Where do you want these?" I asked as a few big drops splatted against the sidewalk.

"Around the garden," he yelled over the sound of thunder. "Where else?"

Frankie bent over, red-faced, and started shoving sandbags around the giant radish plants—that public-challenge crop from which Frankie and I are growing the biggest single radish this town has ever seen. Frankie was working like a teenager.

"Slackard," he snarled as I stood chuckling. "I hope your musk melons drown."

It wasn't really even raining yet and, although the ground was saturated, I didn't anticipate anything of serious consequence in the garden, unless a tree fell on it of course. I went inside to get a beer.

A few minutes later Frankie stomped into the kitchen, just as a thunderclap rattled the windows. Moments later, a torrential downpour let loose from the sky, and within minutes, the entire garden was inundated. The corn was under water, the peas were flooded, and the melons were swamped. Everything but the giant radishes.

Frankie leaned against a wall, grinning smugly, and opened a beer. Water ran down the sidewalk, hit the sandbag dike he'd just built, and poured around the giant radish plants.

"Take a lesson from an old gardener," he said, tipping his beer. "An ounce of protection is worth a pound of cure, he who hesitates is lost, and you always reap what you sow."

"Anything else?" I grumbled, watching my beets float away.

"Yeah," he said. "You're out of beer."

BIG MO RUMBLES IN THE NIGHT

It happened at night, a few days ago. Frankie and I were standing in the kitchen of my apartment and my girlfriend was sitting at the table trying to write something down. Suddenly, the floor began to tremble.

"Yipes!" Frankie yelled. "I think we just had an earthquake."

I listened and stood on the tile floor barefooted. I felt it too. A trembling, a small shaking, a vibrating of the floor.

"Not an earthquake," I said softly. "I think that was Big Mo."

Frankie grabbed a flashlight and flew out the back door.

By the time I got to him, Frankie was squatting over the giant radish bed in the garden behind my house. He had the leaves of Big Mo pulled back and he was shining his flashlight on him.

"My God," Frankie yelled. "He's exploded!"

I pushed my way into the radish patch. Sure enough. It was Big Mo, the biggest of three finalists in our giant radish contest. And he had suffered a concussion-like injury. He had grown so fast, tried so hard, that he split his outer skin, exploded, and apparently shook the earth.

"We'd better get him out of the ground," Frankie said solemnly. "Where can we get a backhoe this time of night?"

I didn't know.

"We've got to be careful," I said. "Samson and Hercules (giant radishes on either side of Big Mo) are still growing. We don't want to disturb them."

"Right," Frankie said. He headed for the garage to get a shovel, some rope and a pulley to take our giant radish from the ground.

It took a lot of digging and pulling, but finally Big Mo came out. He was badly scarred from a season of hard growing. Frankie and I dragged him back to the house and turned on the porch lights.

"It's bigger than I thought it would be," Frankie said softly. "Kind of frightening."

Just then Big Mo rolled slightly in reaction to gravity. Frankie jumped back.

"Look out!" he yelled. "It's still alive."

"No, it isn't," I said. "It just rolled a little." My cat walked by and hissed at it.

"I don't know. Those were Japanese seeds," he said. "Haven't you ever seen Japanese science fiction films about radiation causing mutant things to grow huge and live free?"

"That's just Japanese Hollywood," I said. "What we have here is a giant, contest-winning radish, of enormous proportion."

The next morning Frankie came over with his camera and we took a picture. Giant radishes don't last long in the heat. We wanted to make an official record for the contest that we launched a couple of months ago.

"How will we decide who wins this giant radish contest?" Frankie asked as I snapped the picture. He was trying to hold up the radish with both hands.

"I know a couple of farm guys who will judge this thing for us, if we give them beer," I said. "But they'll have to do it from photographs. Can you imagine trying to take this radish someplace in the car? It'd break a leaf spring."

"Right," said Frankie. "And hurry up with the photograph. It's also breaking my arm."

As you can see in the photo, this is no piker of a radish. And though some might say it looks like a giant turnip, don't believe it. It's a radish, all right.

If anybody out there thinks they've grown a bigger one, take a picture of it and send it in. I suggest you get back a long way to take the picture so you'll be sure to get it all in. I'd start about a block away. That's what Frankie and I had to do.

As far as incentive goes, I will personally have your radish made into a giant trophy if you win.

But I'm not worried. And neither is Frankie.

"We've done it," Frankie said when last we talked. "It's a world beater. But now, what do we do with it?"

I said I didn't know. But later I'm calling somebody with a chain saw and a tow truck to haul it away. Then I just plan to sit back and wait for the challenges to start rolling in. Good luck. And may the biggest radish win.

Before leaving for a lengthy vacation, Luzadder prepared some columns to be published in his absence. Radish contest entries should be sent to him c/o general delivery, Charlevoix, Michigan. - Ed.

FRANKIE'S RADISH LED THE FIELD

This is to announce that I, myself, and my good friend Frankie, have won First Prize in the World's Largest Radish Growing and Bragging About Contest for 1982.

We are proud to announce that we grew the most enormous radish entered in a contest we personally concocted, promoted, entered and judged.

You may remember that the editors of this newspaper, easily excited by giant vegetables, published a picture early in August of me and Frankie's giant radish. And they invited anyone to submit a photo of a bigger garden radish than me and Frankie's.

So, after waiting a full six weeks, we decided it was time to unveil the truth.

We tried to find impartial judges, but everybody we knew was either intoxicated or out of town on judging day.

So, Frankie and I agreed to judge this contest ourselves. To do this, we first took a pledge to be honest.

"Do you solemnly swear to be an honest judge?" I asked Frankie.

He swore out loud and so did I.

"Okay, then," I said. "Let's go take a look at the entries."

Frankie and I went into the kitchen and got out the big manila envelope set aside for all the photos of giant radishes.

"Here," I said to Frankie. "You open the envelope. I'm too nervous to look."

Frankie took the envelope and shook it upside down over the kitchen table. But nothing happened.

He opened it wider and shook it again.

Nothing came out.

"Hey," Frankie yelled. "There's nothing in here."

I grabbed the envelope and peered inside. Sure enough. There wasn't a single photo of a single radish in the entire envelope.

"You mean we didn't get one giant entry?" Frankie said. He was astounded.

I shrugged my shoulders.

"Guess not," I said. "This is the official envelope for the official contest and we're the judges and this is judging day. And I don't see a single entry but ours."

Frankie grabbed a beer from the icebox, took a long drink, pulled himself up to the full height of an official judge, and did his duty.

"Then, by the power invested in me as a judge," he declared, "we 'is' the winners."

I voted it unanimous, we shook hands, and retired to the porch to celebrate our victory.

"You know," Frankie said as we sat in the swing, "it wasn't as tough a contest as I thought it would be. We must have scared 'em with the hugeness of our radish."

"They wouldn't have had a chance even if they had entered," I muttered.

"Now you're right," Frankie said. "What's more, just wait 'til next year. We'll beat nobody again if we have to."

And with that we shook on it again, sat back, and began to relish the sweetness of a landslide victory.

END NOTE

There was no radish contest the following year, but there was a contest to name the newest and tallest building in town, a hideous monstrosity – in Luzadder's estimation – that he described as a "sidewalk to the sky." He took the winners to a restaurant on top of the building – for a hot dog.

Luzadder would leave the News-Sentinel in January, 1984, in the wake of the newspaper's Pulitzer Prize and in which his contributions would later be highlighted in college textbooks as models of how to write feature stories on deadline.

His departure and his decision to move from column writing into investigative reporting would inform his work for the next 30 years in a career that included national recognition from the American Bar Association for public service, a place in the Scripps Howard Journalism Hall of Fame - and a repertoire of unforgettable campfire stories that could put a lasting chill down the back.

Luzadder is the author of two books, both addressing issues in journalism: The Manchurian Journalist, about the media and the domestic propaganda of the Cold War intelligence community, published in June, 2024; and, Guzik's Legacy, the story of the media-driven myth of Al Capone and the true history of the Chicago mob, is awaiting publication. He lives and writes in Oregon, and is my father. — Hannah M. Cowden, Editor and Attorney at Law

ABOUT THE AUTHOR

Photo by Nancy Luzadder

Dan Luzadder is an American journalist and author whose lengthy newspaper career began as a teenaged police reporter in the last days of linotypes. He came of age amid hagiographic newsroom characters who believed shoe leather reporting, tight deadlines and well-placed sources were journalism's divinity. He has written for the New York Daily News and the New York Times, shared a Pulitzer Prize (1983) for general local reporting, won a national public service award from the American Bar Association for exposing corruption in federal courts, and is a member of the Scripps Howard Journalism Hall of Fame. He resides with his wife, Nancy, in the Pacific Northwest. He is currently at work on an investigative documentary series on a cold-case crime spree in Speedway, Indiana in 1978, and is completing a book exploring the American *myth* of Al Capone.

www.ingramcontent.com/pod-product-compliance
Lightning Source LLC
Chambersburg PA
CBHW061158120626
46546CB00005B/2107